SOBIBOR

MARTYRDOM
AND
REVOLT

SOBIBOR

MARTYRDOM AND REVOLT

**Documents and Testimonies
Presented by**

MIRIAM NOVITCH

Preface by Léon Poliakov

HOLOCAUST LIBRARY
NEW YORK

BY THE SAME AUTHOR

Le Droit d'Avoir, Témoignages sur les massacres des Juifs en Pologne. Paris: Rodstein Ed., 1946.

The Jewish Resistance and the Allies, Milan, Italy 1961, (mimeographed).

La Vérité sur Treblinka, Paris: Presses du Temps Présent, 1967.

Israel doit être détruit (La Guerre de Six Jours), Paris: Presses du Temps Présent, 1967.

La Révolte du ghetto de Varsovie, Paris: Presses du Temps Présent, 1968.

L'extermination des Tziganes, Paris: A.M.I.F., 1969.

Le passage des barbares, Préface de Léon Poliakov, Paris: Presses du Temps Présent, 1972.

Le Chant du Peuple Juif Massacré, traduction du Yiddish du poème d'Itzhak Katzenelson, Marseille, 1975 (En collaboration avec Suzanne Der).

Il Canto del Popolo Ebreo Massacrato, Milano: C.D.E.C., 1978. (Tradotto dello Yiddish del Canto di Itzhak Katzenelson, con Fausta Beltrami).

Sobibor, Martyre et Révolte, Préface de Léon Poliakov, Université de Paris 7, 1978.

Sobibor, Martyrdom and Revolt (in Hebrew) Tel-Aviv: Ghetto Fighters' House, 1979.

Resistenza Spirituale — Spiritual Resistance 1940-1945, 120 drawings from Concentration Camps and Ghettos. Published by the "Comune" of Milan. Prefaces: Carlo Tognoli, Mayor of Milan, Moshe Alon, Israel Ambassador in Rome. In two languages, Italian and English, Milan, 1979.

Spiritual Resistance, Art in Concentration Camps and Ghettos, U.A.H.C., New York: 1979.

Miriam Novitch collected the documentary film material used in the production of the movies: *Eichmann and the Third Reich,* Presens Film, Zurich, 1962; *The 81st Blow,* Ghetto Fighters House, 1977.

Publication of this book was made possible
by a grant from Benjamin and Stefa Wald

Cover designed by Eric Gluckman
Printed in the United States of America
by Waldon Press, Inc., New York City

Table of Contents

*"Who, in this world, could reply to
the terrible obstinacy of crime, if not
for the obstinacy of witnessing?"*

Albert Camus (from the preface to
Let My People Go, by Jacques Mery)

PREFACE

Thirty-five years later . . . Yet, even now the Holocaust affects our modern sensibilities in different ways. It is particularly appropriate to consider the pure and simple denial which is still so common, a reaction which seems to be the West's semi-conscious way of shunning its responsibilities rather than an organized "neo-Nazi" ideology. The assumption that the general public is well informed is based on the fact that school books refer to the figure of six million victims. Most people, in reality, do not want to know more than what is to be found in some paperbacks flavored with sadistic eroticism or in those which skirt the real horror. As for school children, according to my observations the event is utterly inconceivable to them . . . But this healthy reaction is an integral part of their typical rejection of the adult world (the "counter-culture" of the youth); this may easily lead an anarchist or fascist fringe group to identify with the nihilists of the Third Reich.

To have the naked truth of the extermination camps accepted is no easy task. With this end in mind, Miriam Novitch, with total self-denial, has dedicated thirty-five years of her life. Yes, more than thirty-five years; I remember when she visited me at my home in Chevreuse after the Nuremberg Trials and showed me the first assortment of survivors' accounts that she had gathered. In the present collection of documents she informs us about one of the six largest death camps, though perhaps the least known· Sobibor, in eastern Poland.

In previous writings, some of which are unpublished, Miriam Novitch examined the steps taken by the executioners.

After 1935, with the promulgation of the Nuremberg Laws, anti-Semitic propaganda was intensified in the Third Reich. Slogans, songs, films, exhibitions were abundant everywhere. In public meetings, as in schools, the nature of the Jew was maligned. Here were laid the foundations of the gas chambers; here were trained the men who without hesitation were to turn on the motors or open the canisters of Zyklon B and suffocate millions of men, women and children.

We might add that, in spite of their inevitable sadistic behavior, most of these men did not take pleasure in carrying out their special task.

Heinrich Himmler, aware of the situation, declared one day at a meeting of SS leaders:

I wish to talk today about the evacuation of the Jews, the extermination of the Jewish people. It is a simple matter for discussion . . . The Jews will be exterminated, it is clear, it is in our program, says every member of our party: elimination of the Jews, extermination, we will do that. And then they come, our 80 million decent Germans, and each one has his "good" Jew. The others, it is clear, are swine, but this one is a first-class Jew. Of all those who speak thus, no one has seen the corpses, no one has gone through it. Most of you know what it means when 100 corpses lie there, or when 500 corpses lie there, or when 1000 corpses lie there. To have gone through this and — apart from a few exceptions caused by human weakness — to have remained decent, that has made us great. (October 1943).

Such remarks suggest the existence of a kind of cruel "collective anti-Semitic super-ego" in the Third Reich. Here is an account of a soldier in the German Army: "In Nowogrodek, extermination was carried out by an SS commando whose idealism enabled them to do their duty without schnaps." We must admit that the new generation of Hitler's admirers, from the American Nazi Party to the young Parisian collectors of Nazi relics, are completely ignorant of this kind of idealism.

Moreover, the truly dedicated SS quickly adapted to their task, especially in the case of the professional killers who, before operating the death camps, had experimented on the inmates of the insane asylums and on other sick people in Germany. The euthanasia program was put into practice by a secret order issued by Hitler on September 1, 1939 as Miriam Novitch tells us:

> The first euthanasia establishment was created in Brandenberg in Prussia in a converted prison. Others followed: at Grafeneck, in Württemberg; at Sonnenstein, in Saxony; at Hadamar, in Hesse; at Bernburg/Saale, in Thuringia, and at Hartheim in Austria. (The two commanders of Sobibor, Franz Stangl and his successor, Frank Reichleitner, both came from Hartheim.)

> The exact number of euthanasia victims is unknown. According to Stangl, 13,000 German patients were put to death in the establishment of Hartheim alone (he mentioned this figure at his trial in Düsseldorf in May 1970).

Due to the pressure of the Churches as well as to public demonstrations which took place near the euthanasia establishments, the leaders of the Third Reich decided to suspend their operations in August 1941. Actually, these were to begin again immediately after the final victory of the war. The specialized euthanasia personnel were thereby designated to implement the "final solution of the Jewish question." Miriam Novitch informs us that there were ninety-two murderers in the program:

> Erwin Lambert, a master carpenter from Stuttgart who had constructed the euthanasia gas chambers at Hartheim, Hadamar and Sonnenstein, was sent to Poland for the same task. He was to disguise the gas chambers at Sobibor as shower stalls, just as he had done in the German establishments. He was to seal them hermetically so that the carbon monoxide gas would not escape and would kill all the victims.

> At first, the ninety-two experts were integrated into an SS detachment, stationed at Trawniki in Poland. After receiving military training, they were separated into three groups of advanced-guard commandos *(Vorkommandos)*, each charged with setting up a death camp: Sobibor and Belzec to the east of Lublin, and Treblinka to the north.

The information gathered by Miriam Novitch enables her to describe with precision the installation and operations of Sobibor: "The construction of Sobibor began at the end of February or the beginning of March, 1942: the *Vorkommando* was directed by SS officer Christian Wirth, one of the first directors of euthanasia. Later, a team of inmates, exempted from immediate death, was assigned the job of enlarging and improving the facilities. In April, 1943, they began to build a casino for the SS; a special cinema was provided for the Ukrainian auxiliary guard.

At this stage, the technical work was directed by private contractors. The commanding officer, Stangl, who arrived in Sobibor on April 28, 1942, supervised the construction. There were five gas chambers, fifty square meters each, and built to hold approximately 2,000 people. The victims entered by a "western door"; the corpses were evacuated by the "eastern door." They were then put on a train, transported to common graves and buried. Later on, they were burned.

The first victims of Sobibor were a group of 150 Jews from Wlodawa, a small nearby village. They were followed by thousands of others from Hrubieszow, Krasnystaw, Mielec and other towns of the region. We learn from survivors that the Polish deportees, who were in the majority, were savagely beaten as they came out of the train; no doubt, this was to assure maximum discipline. By contrast, the deportees from Western countries who, in general, did not suspect the fate which awaited them, were kept in ignorance and were calmly invited to undress before entering the "showers."

The techniques used in the death factories are generally well-known: the public is aware that in the Third Reich Jews were gassed with carbon monoxide in the "Polish camps" and with Zyklon B in Auschwitz, that most advanced establishment. It is likely that Adolf Hitler himself suggested the procedure.[1]

However, the facts about the resistance and uprisings in the camps are still not generallly known; even Jewish readers or people concerned with the history of racial persecutions believe the legend of the six million martyrs who went to their death like "sheep."

The testimony gathered by Miriam Novitch shows us that several attempts to rebel did take place in each of the death camps. Consequently, extermination was interrupted in Sobibor as well as in Treblinka because of successful revolts. These texts disclose important factors underlying the Jewish rebellion. One account is particularly revealing. It is well known that slaves have always tried to revolt. Haim Treger, a survivor, confirms this: "We Jews, the most unfortunate people in the world, have beheaded murderers of children, have put bullets into the heads of scoundrels, into their sadistic skulls." But, beyond this, these men were driven by a will to survive in order to bear witness. This tragic mission left its mark on the majority of survivors, as Herszel Zukerman explains: "To survive Sobibor does not mean to continue living." The leader of the revolt, Lieutenant "Sashka" Pechersky, expressed it in a different way: "We are not allowed to give up life, we must live in order to take our revenge."

The revolt of October 14, 1943 was carefully prepared in utmost secrecy by a handful of inmates, but with the aim of allowing the largest possible number of prisoners to survive in order to transmit testimony. We shall return to this subject in the accounts which follow, particularly those pertaining to Lieutenant Pechersky and other active participants. We will see what other tribulations awaited the victorious rebels; in occupied Poland, survival in the forests imposed a continual struggle, just as it did in the camps.

Miriam Novitch gives us further statistical and ethnological information:

As for the number of victims, the Commission investigating Nazi war crimes in Poland cites the following figures:

Belzec - 600,000 victims
Sobibor - 250,000 victims
Treblinka - 800,000 victims

In the case of Sobibor, the testimony of survivors suggests that the figure of 250,000 victims is lower than the actual one. As in Treblinka, many groups of Gypsies were gassed here, along with the Jews.

In 1967, I visited the site of the death camp of Sobibor and found some objects belonging to the victims which had been buried in stone-pits or in moss. I collected them with the same fervor as I did the testimony which follows. The objects will gradually disappear. But the accounts will remain.

I hope that these tragic pages will continue to serve as a warning to mankind that the day will come when discrimination, genocide and war will disappear and that Peace — Shalom — the dream of our prophets will be established in the whole world.

Since so few witnesses have survived, let us have the patience to listen to all of them despite their tediousness and repetition. To listen to them is to pay homage not only to the martyrs and fighters of Sobibor but to all of those who experienced the Nazi infernos.

Léon Poliakov

[1]In *Mein Kampf*, written by Hitler in 1924, one finds the following statement at the end: "If, at the beginning, or during the war, twelve or fifteen hundred of these Hebraic corrupters of our people had been asphyxiated by gas . . . the sacrifice of millions of soldiers would not have been in vain." (462nd edition, 1939, pg. 772).

INTRODUCTION

Before Sobibor

Anti-Semitism was a state doctrine in Germany well before the Second World War. For many Nazi propagandists it became the integral part of their philosophy of life" *(Weltanschauung)*. The famous slogan *"Die Juden sind unser Unglück"* (Jews are our misfortune) became the creed of politicians and intellectuals. From time immemorial, the Jewish people have been the ideal scapegoat for the greedy and the unscrupulous and those whose life proved unsuccessful. Anti-Semitism was to lead Nazi Germany to Sobibor. Among the personnel of Sobibor we find doctors, musicians and civil servants, as well as ordinary workers and peasants.

Hitler and his party came to power on January 30, 1933. The surest means to fulfill a cherished plan was to extirpate the racially inferior Jews from the German body politic. *(Die rassisch Minderwertigen aus dem deutschen Volkskörper ausmerzen)*.

To begin with, it was vital to exclude Jews from public life (Decree of April 7, 1933, RGBL I.S. 175ff. *Reichsbürgergesetz* of September 15, 1935, RGBL I.S. 1146).

By the decree for the "Protection of German blood and German honor" *(Gesetz zum Schutze des deutschen Blutes und der deutschen Ehre)* of September 15, 1935, a German had no right to marry a Jewess, nor a Jew to wed a German woman.

After 1935, anti-Semitic propaganda was intensified; a large amount of money was spent on slogans, songs, films (with the participation of talented artists), and documentary exhibitions. At public meetings, adults, young people and even children were taught the wickedness of the Jews. That is how the foundations were laid for the future gas chambers; people were trained so that they would have no human feelings at Belzec, Sobibor, Treblinka, and would unhesitatingly open canisters of Zyklon B gas. Men, women and children were to die only because they were Jews.

Without the slightest emotion anti-Semitic propagandists would watch crowds of tortured prisoners walking to their death. Anti-Semitism was to smother pity and fellow feeling in apparently good people. They were to become callous to Jewish martyrdom, and would join the accomplices of the crimes committed at Sobibor.

Crystal Night

The first poisoned fruit of anti-Semitic propaganda was Crystal Night, on November 9-10, 1938.

A young Jew, Herszel Grynszpan, decided to react to the wave of lies and injustice. His family, who lived in Hanover, had been deported. Herszel killed a German, Ernst von Rath, who was employed in the German Embassy in Paris. Here was an excellent pretext for the Nazis to convert the words of hatred into acts of violence and murder.

On the night of November 9, 1938, at the instigation of Goebbels, the minister of propaganda, the SA and SS launched a brutal assault against the German Jewish population. Shops and houses were ransacked, synagogues destroyed. A ransom of a billion marks (equivalent to 400 million dollars) was imposed on the Jewish community.[2] At the same time, 20,000 Jews were arrested and deported to the first concentration camps of Dachau and Buchenwald.[3]

Young Herszel, who was sent to prison in France, was to be handed over to the Nazis by the Vichy police, in 1940. After a stay in Sachsenhausen, he was traced to Magdeburg prison.[4] Then he disappeared.

In 1938, Jews tried to flee this regime of thieves and murderers, but where could they go? The United States? South America? These borders were shut. Only the wealthy, some intellectuals and celebrities were to find refuge outside Nazi Germany. But the poor masses of Germany, Poland, and the Baltic States had no place to go. They were to remain with the tyrants, and later be deported to the death camps, along with some intellectuals and businessmen who had fled Germany in 1938 and 1939 and found refuge in France and Holland. In 1942-1943, they were arrested everywhere; more than 30,000 Dutch Jews died in Sobibor.

"Where shall we go? The doors are shut,

"And all the roads are blocked . . ."   was the refrain of an anonymous Yiddish song from that time.

In accordance with the decree of July 4, 1939, applied in Germany and the territories occupied by the *Wehrmacht,* Jews would come under the administration of the notorious R.S.H.A. (Reich Security Main Office).

On September 1, 1939, Germany invaded Poland, and on June 22, 1941, attacked Russia, both of them countries with large Jewish populations. We do not know exactly when the first order for the "Final Solution" of the Jewish question was given; it is assumed that it took place in the spring of 1941, before the attack on Russia, and at the time when the *Einsatzgruppen* (special killing commandos) were created. Eichmann's trial in Jerusalem gave us the date of September, 1939, which is probably the correct one.

During the Nuremberg trials, General Erwin Lahousen, of the German counter-espionage agency, affirmed that, as of September, 1939, Hitler had decided to massacre the Jews. His decision was well known among his henchmen, but details for its execution were not ready. This was revealed by Heydrich at a meeting organized on the 27 of September, 1939, four weeks after the declaration of war. On September 21, Heydrich sent an express letter containing advice regarding mass extermination. That letter, as well as the report of the meeting on the 27th of September were shown to Eichmann during his trial.[5] Both documents mention the "Final Solution," but the decision was to be kept secret. Eichmann attended that meeting on the 27 of September and his name was among those present. He confessed: "After having read those documents, I think that the extermination orders were not given by Hitler at the start of the Russian-German war, but the idea materialized at the same time as the following decrees were proclaimed:

1. Polish Jews were to be transferred to big cities;
2. German Jews were to be sent to Poland."

We must add that the following participants at the meeting on the 27th of September played an active role in the gas chamber killings:

— General SS Otto Ohlendorf, chief of *Einsatzgruppe D*, who confessed to the shooting of 90,000 Jews;

— Colonel SS Josef Walter Rauff, specialist in gas chambers;

— General SS Arthur Nebe, Commander of the *Einsatzgruppe B*;

— Colonel SS Damzog, the Gestapo chief of Warthegau, where the first death camp at Chelmno was built;

— General SS Bruno Streckenbach, former police chief;

— General SS Erich Naumann, Commander of *Einsatzgruppe C*;

— Eichmann and associates, guilty of the crime of genocide.

After the occupation of Poland, Hitler signed a decree ordering the formation of a General Government incorporating the districts of Cracow, Radom, Warsaw, Lublin and Galicia. Dr. Hans Frank became governor general, and Dr. Joseph Bühler his aide; both were fanatic anti-Semites.

The Government General controlled an area of 53,000 square miles with a population of 20 million, including 2½ million Jews.

Before the massacres began, there was a virulent campaign of anti-Jewish propaganda, and the authorities took discriminatory measures against the Jewish population.

On November 23, 1939, the six-pointed-star badge appeared, all Jews had to wear it and Jewish establishments had to display it. By the two decrees of November 20, 1939 and March 1, 1940, Jewish funds were blocked in the banks. The law of December 16, 1939 banned Jews from employing gentiles, and they could no longer receive Social Security benefits.

On January 24, 1940, all Jews were forced to declare all of their possessions, and, as of January 26, they were not allowed to travel by train. Jews between the ages of fourteen and sixty were registered for forced labor.

Finally, by the decrees of September 13, 1940, August 29, and October 15, 1941, Jews were forbidden to change their residence, under the penalty of death.

In May, 1940, the police schools of Pretsch-on-Elbe, Duenen and Schmiedeberg were used to form the four *Einsatzgruppen*

A, B, C, D, whose duties were to carry out the mass murder of Jews and other enemies of the regime. Propagandists portrayed Jews at their vilest, and Jews had no power to defend themselves against these lies. Rosenberg and his gang circulated widely the "Protocols of the Elders of Zion," a slanderous book written under the Tsar.

As of June 22, 1941, SS commandos followed the regular army, and hundreds of thousands of innocent people were to be murdered in fields, ditches and forests. They were forced to undress under the supervision of the SS policemen or soldiers of the *Wehrmacht,* whips in hand. Many documents describing these mass shootings have been published, including those of German witnesses, such as that of Graebe, on the extermination of Jews in the town of Dubno.

In the occupied territories in Russia, Jews were massacred in ravines and in woods. But this seemed inadequate in the eyes of the murderers: they needed more efficient measures to annihilate millions of Jews. In January, 1942, at the infamous Wannsee conference, it was decided to murder eleven million Jews. At his trial, Eichmann testified that it was not a question whether Jews should be killed or not, but how to exterminate them all.

Concentration First

Following the recommendations of Heydrich at the conference of September 27, 1939, Polish Jews were to be concentrated in large cities and German Jews were to be evacuated to Poland. They were to be interned in districts accessible to railway stations, in order to facilitate the task of future deportations to the death camps. Warsaw would thus have a concentration of 500,000 people and was to be the assembly point, not only for Jews from the neighboring districts but for those from Germany, as well. As we shall see in the following pages, Jews deported from Germany, Austria and Czechoslovakia were sent to Polish towns. In the spring of 1942, these deported Jews were among the first victims of Sobibor, Belzec and Treblinka.

The Death Machine Is Set In Motion

On July 31, 1941, Göring wrote to Heydrich as follows: "To help in the achievement of the task which was entrusted to you in the decree dated January 21, 1939 to solve the Jewish question by emigration and evacuation in the most favorable way possible, given the conditions of that time — I herewith commission you to carry out all necessary arrangements, whether organizational, substantive, or financial, for a total solution of the Jewish question in the German sphere of influence in Europe.

"I further commission you to submit to me promptly an overall plan showing the preliminary organizational, substantive, and financial measures for the execution of the intended final solution of the Jewish question."[7]

Following Göring's orders, Heydrich began the construction of the death camps. After his execution by Czechoslovakian patriots on June 5, 1942, the extermination action and the confiscation of the victims' possessions was called "Operation or *Einsatz* Reinhard."

The role played by the SS in the mass killings is well known. *Reichsführer* Heinrich Himmler personally supervised "Operation Reinhard". He visited Sobibor and other death camps and signed orders concerning deportations, using the term *Umsiedlung* (resettlement) to hide the truth.

The Police Forces and the Final Solution

Police forces in the Government General were under the orders of the Higher SS and Police Leaders *(Höhere SS und Polizeiführer, HSSPF)*, who were under the direct order of Himmler. The highest in command of the SS and the police between October, 1939 and November, 1943 was SS *Obergruppenführer* Friedrich Krüger. He was later replaced by Wilhelm Koppe, from November, 1943 to January, 1945. Both were headquartered in Cracow.[8] Also under SS control was BdO *(Befehlshaber der Ordnungpolizei,* Commander of the Security Police).

To enable the Nazi violence to succeed, the SS and the police leaders were placed in five Polish districts: Warsaw, Radom, Cracow, Galicia and Lublin. There they were assisted by commanders in the order and security service. These people served Operation Reinhard by hunting down Jews and sending them to the death camps. Escape was almost impossible. The few survivors will testify for those who no longer have any voice.

By the time the death camps were constructed, SS *Oberführer* Scherner had replaced Schwendler, who had been deemed unequal to the task. Next came SS General Böttcher. He replaced SS General Katzmann, a man known for his violence, who was sent to Galicia, a region with a large Jewish population.

SS General Dr. von Sammern Frankenegg was sent to Warsaw where he remained during the mass deportations and the revolt of April 1943.[9] While the three *Oberführers* Schwendler, Wiegand and Oberg were leaving Poland, the SS and police leader in Lublin, formerly the *Gauleiter* of Vienna Odilo Globocnik, remained, and took charge of *Operation Reinhard*. Globocnik created a special section for the "Final Solution," under the direction of SS *Sturmbannführer* Hermann Hoefle.[10]

Under Hoefle's command was SS *Oberführer* Christian Wirth, a policeman from Stuttgart, who was to supervise the construction of the death camps and become inspector of Belzec, Sobibor and Treblinka. His title was "Inspector of special commandos of Operation Reinhard". His subordinates nicknamed him "The Savage Christian" *(Der wilde Christian)* because of his lust for murder. Jankiel Wiernik, who escaped from Treblinka, describes Wirth as a man of fifty, with a short beard and a pince-nez. Wirth's associate, SS Josef Oberhauser, was also to rule Belzec; after the war, he was tried in East Germany for his activities in the field of euthanasia. Because there were no witnesses left alive, he was not tried for his crimes in Belzec; the only survivor, Rudolph Reder, an engineer from Lvov, was dead.

Globocnik, as chief of the SS and the police, acted under the orders of the Supreme chief of the SS and the police. However, Globocnik worked directly with Himmler and the General of the Waffen SS Karl Wolf.[11]

The builders and personnel of Operation Reinhard belonged mainly to the euthanasia team. They constructed the three death camps of Belzec, Sobibor and Treblinka, which became the apparatus of mass murder.

Euthanasia began in Germany at the start of the war, and targeted human beings "unworthy to live" *(lebensunwertigen Leben)*, that is, mentally ill, physically handicapped and incurable people. Nazi leaders took advantage of the war to commit homicide, believing that public opinion would remain silent. They were wrong, a German life was still important to the public opinion.

At the head of the euthanasia program was SS *Reichsführer* Heinrich Himmler, assisted by Philip Bouhler, chief of Hitler's Chancellery as well as Hitler's private doctor, Karl Brand. In 1945, Bouhler committed suicide; Brand was condemned to death by an American court and executed in 1948.

On Hitler's Service

Hitler and his party were never short of so-called intellectuals: Professors Heyde, Nietsche, Pfannenstiel, Krantz and many others were very active in the field of euthanasia. Krantz estimated in an article in *NS Volksdienst* (April 1940), that Germany had a million such useless people who should be eliminated. Film producers made a movie of that period in which they emphasized the benefits that Germany would realize once it got rid of these non-productive elements. According to them, the percentage of the mentally ill among Jews was excessively high.[12]

We do not find these "professors" at Sobibor, but their disciples were there, fully justified morally and intellectually for the dreadful crimes that they were committing.

The same SS *Scharführer* Erwin Lambert, a carpenter from Stuttgart who built the gas chambers for euthanasia in Hadamar, Hartheim and Sonnenstein, was sent to Poland for the same "mission" and then to Trieste, Italy, in 1943. He was to camouflage the gas chambers of Sobibor as showers, and to seal them hermetically to prevent the escape of carbon monoxide. Professional male nurses from euthanasia establishments, experts in the profession of murder, were also sent to Poland, as well as incinerators *(Brenner)*.

The mentally ill and other "useless" people were unaware of the fate awaiting them; they were given sleeping drugs and morphia injections. The inmates of Sobibor were simply told: "You are going to have a disinfecting shower in order to avoid epidemics before your long journey to the Ukraine." If these words did not calm the victims, whippings and beatings were used, according to the testimony of the escaped prisoner, Jankiel Wiernik, at the first Treblinka trial in Düsseldorf, 1965.

The first euthanasia establishment was created in Brandenburg, Prussia, in an abandoned prison. Others followed in Grafeneck, Münstigen, Württemberg, in Sonnenstein near Pirma, Saxony, in Hadamar, district of Limburg in Hessen, in Bernburg/Saale in Thuringia as well as Hartheim, Austria, in an old castle near Linz. The two commanders of Sobibor, Franz Stangl and his successor, Franz Reichleitner, came from Hartheim.

Nobody knows the exact figure of the victims of euthanasia, but it is estimated at 70,000. In Hartheim alone, according to Stangl, 13,000 sick people were killed. Stangl cited that figure at his trial in Düsseldorf in May, 1970.

Under pressure especially from the Protestant church, the leaders of the Reich were forced to postpone mass euthanasia until the post-war period, but, according to Victor Brack, abnormal children were killed throughout the whole period of the war. Alfons Klein, co-director of Hadamar, said at his trial in 1946 that 3,000 incurables were gassed during the war.

After the specialized personnel of euthanasia were deprived of their sinister employment, the T4 offices were put at Globocnik's disposal for Operation Reinhard.

One of the letters shown at the first Treblinka trial, and sent by Globocnik on November 27, 1943, notes that ninety-two specialists of T4 were under his orders.

In the autumn of 1941 and the spring of 1942, euthanasia experts were sent to Poland to the camp of Trawniki, near Lublin, where they received military training.[13]

These experts were separated into three groups, forming the base commandos, whose task it was to build the three death camps: Belzec, near Tomaszow-Lubelski, south of Lublin; Sobibor, near the village of the same name and eight kilometers from Wlodawa, east of Lublin; and Treblinka, on the railway line between Warsaw-Bialystok, southeast of Ostrow-Mazowiecki, near Malkinia.

A State Secret

Euthanasia was treated as a state secret, and all its participants were sworn to silence. Operation Reinhard was also a state secret; men who had not taken a vow of silence in Berlin, had to do so in Trawniki. They signed the following proclamation: "Any member belonging to the team of the death camps swears that he has been instructed by *Sturmbannführer* Hoefle, commander of the head office of Operation Reinhard not to reveal any information, oral or written, on the resettlement of Jews." It was stressed that anyone divulging a secret would be severely punished; it was also forbidden to take photographs of the camp.

The Construction of Sobibor

The construction of Sobibor began at the end of February or in early March, 1942. The initial work was done by one of the Trawniki commandos, under the direction of Christian Wirth. A doctor and a chemist assisted him. Later on, the camp had a casino for the officers, and a cinema for the Ukrainian guards was planned. The work was done by private architects, with the help of the Polish and Jewish forced labor. On April 28, 1942, Franz Stangl arrived in Sobibor, bringing building material and a large amount of money for the purchase of additional material. From that day on, Stangl supervised all construction.

Each new chamber was ten meters square, and had two doors, one on the east and one on the west. The victims entered by the western door, the dead were evacuated by the eastern one. Bodies were piled up on wagons and sent to common graves or incinerated.

At the beginning, the dead were buried in graves, thirty meters by fifteen, and four or five meters deep. Beginning with the winter of 1942, they were no longer buried, but were burned in large open crematoria.

The camp was surrounded by barbed wire, a belt of mines and a ditch filled with water. Sobibor was the only death camp that was mined.

The first victims of Belzec (the first death camp) were the 30,000 Jews of the old community of Lublin. The first victims of Sobibor were 150 Jews deported from Wlodawa. They were followed by thousands of Jews from Hrubieszow, Mielec and Krasnystaw.

The executioners used gas or bullets. As we shall see later, the sick, the invalids, and those who dared to resist, were shot.

The Camp Organization

The *Hauptsturmführer* Richard Thomalla was the first commander of the camp. His fate is unknown, and he is believed to have died in 1957. His name was mentioned in the Majdanek camp trial. The second commander was Franz Stangl, who came to the camp on April 28, 1942 and stayed three months. His family lived nearby in the village of Sobibor in a nice property by a lake. He was later sent to Treblinka, where he was to be commander until the revolt of August 2, 1943. Finally he was sent to Italy. He was replaced at Sobibor by Franz Reichleitner who died after the war, without a trial.

Each of the three camp sections had a *Lagerführer,* who supervised the Ukrainian guard and the prisoners who were condemned to hard labor *(Arbeitshäftlinge).* The Ukrainians themselves were divided into groups of six men under the command of a *Volksdeutsche* (a Ukrainian of German origin). The prisoners were divided into groups led by the Kapos.

At first, the SS personnel had no specific tasks, but with the improvement of the murder apparatus, each SS officer was given a special function. When a convoy arrived, most of the SS were waiting at the station: 50 to 100 Germans, and 150 to 200 Ukrainians.

The camp occupied an area of fifty-eight hectares and was situated on the Chelm-Wlodawa railway line. The southern spur led directly to the camp, and the rail lines were 500 meters away from the gas chambers. At the end of the camp there was a platform four hundred meters long. At the side of the platform was the *Vorlager,* or living area of the camp personnel. Later the camp was reinforced, under the direction of Stangl.

The Camp Quarters and Their Uses

The camp was divided into a *Vorlager* and four sections, separated by barbed wire. Here is a brief description given by survivors:

In section No. 1 or *Lager No. 1* were the barracks for those prisoners who temporarily were allowed to live, the workshops and the kitchens; section 2, at the end of the *Vorlager* was used for the disrobing of the prisoners, and the storage of belongings left by the victims; the third section had three gas chambers, each of which could hold fifty people.

In 1942, a decision was taken to expand the gas chambers. The SS *Scharführers* Erwin Lambert[14] and Lorenz Hackenholt worked under the leadership of Christian Wirth, SS Kurt Gomerski and Erich Bauer, who were part of the team. At the Sobibor trial, Lambert and Gomerski confessed that this construction took three weeks. Five Ukrainian carpenters and a group of prisoners were also recruited to work.

In order to build the new gas chambers, old houses were pulled down and new ones were erected, each 4×12 meters. Five rooms were prepared to hold 70 to 80 people. Thus, 400 victims could be put to death at the same time, if children were included.[15]

The Hospital

Upon their arrival, the ailing, the infirm and children who had been deported without their families were led to camp No. 3, where there was a ditch. That section was called the "hospital" (Lazaret). The victims were machine-gunned near the ditch by Ukrainian guards, under German supervision. At first, the victims walked to the execution place; in 1942, when the new railway was built, the prisoners were packed into open trucks, and driven to the "hospital."

In the next chapters we shall learn more about Sobibor; let us only say that a very small number of prisoners were allowed to live. In Auschwitz, in spite of the annihilation program, 10 to 25% of the inmates were spared and sent to work in nearby factories.

At Sobibor, only a handful of young men were left to work in the camp itself.

In the summer of 1943, when the convoys from Western Europe increased, small groups of prisoners, exhausted by excruciating work conditions, were taken back to Sobibor and exterminated.

Himmler's Visit to the Camp

Himmler often travelled to inspect this domain of crime. He visited Treblinka on August 15, 1942, and on the 9th of June he went to Warsaw, accompanied by the General of Waffen SS Karl Wolf.[16]

On February 12, 1943, he came to Sobibor with a group of high officers. At the Hagen trial, the eleven members of the personnel of Sobibor said that in order to welcome Himmler and show him the death procedure, the commander ordered that 200 attractive young Jewish women and girls be selected. They were forced to undress in camp No. 2 and were taken to camp No. 3 where they were received by the *Oberscharführer* Erich Bauer, nicknamed the *Bademeister* (the bath attendant), who led them to the gas chambers. On that occasion, as an old fighter of the First World War and a member of the *Stahlhelm,* Bauer put on his best uniform. All the other SS polished their boots, as we learned from the survivors.

The Trains

The victims were brought to Sobibor in freight trains; there were also some passenger trains from West Germany and Holland; others came by lorries, carts, or even on foot.

Each convoy consisted of a minimum of twenty wagons, but some convoys like those heading for Treblinka and Belzec, numbered sixty wagons. Each wagon would hold one hundred people.

On its arrival, the convoy stopped at the entrance of the Vorlager. Here are some details about the reception of the prisoners, given by survivors. The Polish Jews were beaten up, but those from Western countries were treated gently and were assured by an SS man that they were in a transit camp.

All preparations regarding the convoys for Sobibor, Belzec and Treblinka were made by the Eastern Railways, the Gedob, under the direction of Dr. Albert Ganzenmüller, Secretary of State at the Ministry of Transport.[17]

The exchange of letters between Ganzenmüller and Karl Wolf concerning the two daily convoys from Warsaw to Treblinka with 5,000 men, women and children belonging to the "Chosen People", is well known; it was mentioned at the trial of Karl Wolf in Munich, in 1964. Here is a letter from Ganzenmüller to Wolf, concerning Sobibor:

Secret!

Distinguished Party member Wolf!

Following our telephone conversation of July 16, 1942, I enclose the following information from the Director of the Eastern Railways in Cracow. Ever since July 22, 1942, a train with 5,000 Jews has left Warsaw daily for Treblinka, via Malkinia; twice a week, another train with 5,000 Jews, has traveled from Przemysl to Belzec.[18] The Gedob is in constant touch with the Security Service of Cracow.

The massacres at Sobibor began in April, 1942; they stopped for a time because of work on the railways and the construction of the new gas chambers. Each convoy that was directed to Sobibor was issued several written reports: one was sent to the Reich Security Main Office (RSHA) in Berlin; another to the chief of the Security police in Cracow (BdS); a third to the chief of the SS and the police of Lublin (SSPF), General Globocnik.

Lives and Possessions

Besides the crime of homicide, Operation Reinhard was also guilty of pillaging. The survivors of Sobibor remember the "recycling" technique of the belongings of the murdered prisoners. The same procedure took place in every camp. Here are details of the huge income of Sobibor, Belzec and Treblinka. Endless documents on the subjects were shown at the trials of Treblinka and

Sobibor. A note signed by Globocnik, chief of Operation Reinhard and addressed to SS *Sturmbannführer* Hermann Hoefle, director of the Administration Bureau of Lublin and to SS *Oberscharführer* Alois Rzepa, the cashier, gives us the following information:

Zlotys, Reichsmarks in notes	RM 73,852,080.74
Precious metals	8,973,651.60
Foreign banknotes	4,521,224.13
Gold coins	1,736,554.12
Jewels (metal and precious stones)	43,662,450.00
Textiles	46,000,000.00
	RM 178,745,960.59

Globocnik gives us other figures: In a report dated November 4, 1943, he mentioned the staggering amount of RM 100,047,-983.91 (the general did not omit even the pfennigs!). Himmler sent him a letter of thanks on November 30, 1943.

On January 5, 1944, Globocnik, already in Trieste, dispatched to his chief a final detailed report, giving the amount of RM 178,-000,000.00. At the same time, he asked for a reward for some of his men who had been particularly devoted to duty, suggesting the Iron Cross first and second class. He particularly recommended Franz Stangl, first commander of Sobibor and second commander of Treblinka.

The profits of Operation Reinhard were transferred to the Deutsche Reichsbank and the Ministry of the Reich Economy. Gold and jewelry were sent directly to the Führer's Chancellery in Berlin. Prisoners' clothing, from which the yellow star badges, and all signs indicating their origin, were removed, went to several German institutions.

According to Spies and Gnichwitz, the prosecutors at the first and second Treblinka trials, this camp made a "profit" of 100 million marks; Belzec and Sobibor made 78 million.

The treasurer of Sobibor was SS *Scharführer* Beckmann, who was later killed in the revolt of October 14, along with twenty other murderers.

The Revolt of October 14, 1943

Sobibor functioned for eighteen months, from April 1942, to October 1943, when the revolt broke out. It had been carefully prepared under the command of Alexander Aronovich Pechersky, also known as Sashka, who had been deported from Minsk. Leon Feldhendler also played an important role. His father was the rabbi of the town of Zolkiewka. The survivors will narrate this remarkable exploit, as thirty escaped prisoners managed to survive.

On July 5, 1943, Himmler conceived the idea of transforming Sobibor into a concentration and labor camp, and to serve as a depot for arms taken from the enemy. In a letter dated July 15, 1943, SS General Oswald Pohl (Chief of the Service of Administration and Economy), which controlled the concentration camps, discouraged the project.

> July 15, 1943.
> *Reichsführer!*
> Following your order that the transit camp of Sobibor in the district of Lublin should be transformed into a concentration camp, I had a talk on the subject with SS *Gruppenführer* Globocnik. Your aim to install in Sobibor a depot for arms taken from the enemy can be achieved without transformation; we prefer that everything stays as before. Please let me know your answer, which is important for General Globocnik and myself.
>
> Heil Hitler![19]

From July, 1943 on, Russian prisoners were to be used for the construction of barracks destined for the recycling of arms.

On October 14, 1943, the revolt of Sobibor broke out, following the Treblinka uprising of August 2. Maltreated and terrorized prisoners took arms against the powerful masters of Europe.

At that time, Globocnik was no longer Chief of Police and of the SS in Lublin, having already been transferred to Trieste, in Italy. He was replaced by SS General Jacob Sporrenberg. Determined to crush the revolt in Sobibor, he asked and received help from the Wehrmacht and the Luftwaffe.

Sporrenberg ordered cruel reprisals. Rebels caught escaping in the neighboring forests were killed on the spot or brought back to the camp where they were tortured and then executed. A survivor, Esther Raab, got a description of what happened from a Ukrainian woman in Chelm in 1945.

Soon after the uprising, the camp installations were dismantled. Wehrmacht engineers blew up with dynamite the gas chambers, prisoners' barracks and SS villas. Treblinka, after the revolt of August 2, 1943, continued to function until October, and small convoys of people were still put to death there.

Belzec stopped operating in June or July, 1943. The exact date is not known, as the last victims of Belzec were all murdered.

The cleaning up operations of Sobibor were carried out by thirty Jewish prisoners who were sent there from another camp. In November they were murdered near a wood in groups of five and their bodies incinerated. Among them were women. The SS men Juehrs and Zierke who were present at the executions, testified at the Hagen trial.

When everything was all cleaned up, they plowed the earth and planted young pine trees. When we visited Sobibor, we saw a small forest in whose midst was a moving monument representing a man near the charred remains of a child.

After the uprising of Treblinka, 200 prisoners were temporarily spared, that number to be reduced afterwards to thirty. Their martydom was described on November 4, 1964, during the first Treblinka trial. One of the murderers, Mentz, said: "The thirty prisoners were led to the woods in groups of five; kneeling with their heads bent, they were shot with automatic pistols. Before dying, each group was forced to burn the dead of the preceding group."

Peaceful Farms . . .

Operation Reinhard was officially ended on October 19, 1943, as was mentioned in a letter from Globocnik to Himmler. Following Globocnik's advice, farms were to be built on the site of the three death camps and farmers were paid to take care of them.

In Treblinka, we still find traces of the foundations of buildings intended for farm dwellings.

Globocnik's plan, however, did not materialize; at the end of autumn 1943, Hitler's Germany began to crumble.

The Harvest Feast

Fearing new uprisings, the SS ordered the massacres of prisoners in the camps of Majdanek, Trawniki and Poniatowa, where the survivors of the Warsaw ghetto were interned. 18,000 in Majdanek, 14,000 in Poniatowa, and 10,000 in Trawniki were all slaughtered on the 3rd and 4th of November, 1943, in an operation called "Harvest Feast" *(Erntefest)*. In all three camps, prisoners were, indeed, preparing a revolt, encouraged by the uprisings of Warsaw and the other camps. The Trawniki inmates had intended to escape to the forests and join the Resistance, under the orders of Zemsta, a famous partisan. In Poniatowa, arms had been smuggled in by the Jewish resistance in Warsaw. Before being put to death, the prisoners managed to set fire to their barracks and burn all their belongings.

In December, 1943, Commander Franz Reichleitner and some SS men and Ukrainian guards, along with their wives, were sent to occupied Italy. In Trieste, a concentration camp was erected in an old rice factory. Massacres took place and the camp became a gathering place for Jews arrested in Trieste and Venice before being sent to Germany. The deportations lasted until January 1945. San Saba also became a depot for looted Jewish goods and for the imprisonment and execution of Italian and Yugoslav partisans.

In Italy, the men of Operation Reinhard were split into three groups: R1, R2 and R3, stationed respectively in Trieste, Udine and Fiume. According to inquiries made by the Italian police after the war, San Saba had 3,000 victims. The crematorium was built by Erwin Lambert who had constructed the gas chambers in Sobibor and Treblinka. Documents about San Saba contain the names of members of Operation Reinhard: Globocnik, Stangl, Lorenz Hackenholt, Josef Oberhauser and many others.[20]

250,000 Victims

The Commission for the Investigation of Nazi Crimes in Poland gives the following figures:

Belzec: 600,000 victims.
Sobibor: 250,000 victims.
Treblinka: 800,000 victims.

In regard to Belzec, there is no remaining eyewitness to confirm exactly the number of victims. Calculations are based on the number of Jewish residents in the neighboring towns who were deported to Belzec. Based on investigations made in Poland, it is estimated that 800,000 Jews perished in Treblinka. This figure is probably correct and it is engraved on the mausoleum which was built on the site of the camp in 1964.

As for Sobibor, the figure of 250,000 dead is less than accurate. All we know are the exact dates of the arrival of the convoys from Holland.[21] As in Treblinka, many groups of Gypsies were also murdered in Sobibor.[22] It is estimated by historians that over 500,000 Gypsies were murdered by the Nazis.

When we visited Sobibor after the war, we gathered some objects which belonged to the victims, and which had been buried in the woods and the sand. We collected them with the same fervor as we did the testimonies which follow. Time will erase the traces of the abandoned objects; human testimony will remain.

We hope that these tragic tales will serve as a warning to men, so that there will be an end to discrimination, genocide and wars, and that Peace — Shalom — the dream of our ancient prophets, will rule our planet. And since so few witnesses have survived, let us have the patience to listen to them all, in spite of longueurs and repetitions. To listen to them is to render homage not only to our martyrs and fighters of Sobibor but of all the Nazi Inferno.

MIRIAM NOVITCH
Kibbutz of Ghetto Fighters
1960-1973

[2]Testimony of Goering. *Trial of the Major War Criminals,* Vol. IX, pages 276-278. See also Hilberg, page 24.

[3]One of the SS men of Sobibor was Hans Heinz Schütt. He took part in the pogrom on Crystal Night. He was sentenced to three years in prison. He testified at the second Treblinka trial at Düsseldorf, July 1970.

[4]Sworn evidence of the Nazi judge Lutz, witness at the trial of Diewerge (Goebbels' collaborator) at Essen, in February 1967.

[5]Documents T 164 and 165, Leon Poliakov, *Trial in Jerusalem,* (Paris, 1963).

[6]After the war, Hans Frank was condemned to death and executed in 1946. Bühler, a participant in the conference of Wannsee, was executed in Poland in 1948.

[7]Leon Poliakov, *The Trial in Jerusalem* (Paris, 1963), pp. 158-159.

[8]The fate of Krüger is not clear; it seems that he fell on the battlefield in the East. Koppe was not judged; he was living in West Germany where he owned a chocolate factory.

[9]During the ghetto revolt of April 19, 1943, he was replaced by the infamous general SS Jürgen Stroop, charged to crush the Jewish revolt.

[10]Born on June 19, 1911, he was one of the main leaders of the mass killings. He committed suicide in Vienna in 1962.

[11]Accused of complicity in the murder of 300,000 Jews, he was condemned in Munich to fifteen years in prison. He was freed soon thereafter.

[12]Excerpts of this film were used by Erwin Leiser and Miriam Novitch for their documentary *Eichmann and the Third Reich,* produced by Praesens Film, Zurich, 1962. In spring 1941, the film society, Tobis, justified euthanasia, under the title *J'Accuse,* a sentimental story of a professor who killed his wife for the sake of love.

[13]It was an old camp for Soviet prisoners, most of whom died of hunger. It became a training center for the Ukrainian guards and a camp for 10,000 Jews of Warsaw, who were to be murdered on November 3, 1943.

[14]Lambert was sentenced to four years in prison; Hackenholt was not judged. Bauer, recognized by Esther Raab and Lerner, got a life sentence.

[15]At Treblinka, ten gas chambers were built instead of three, but the first gas chambers remained, unlike Sobibor.

[16]Trial of Karl Wolf, Munich 1964.

[17]Ganzenmüller became an engineer at Dortmund after the war. In April, 1973, his trial began at Düsseldorf. He was declared too ill to stand trial and it was stopped.

[18]Document produced by the prosecutors, Spiess and Gnichwitz, at the first Treblinka trial, Düsseldorf.

[19]Document presented at the trial of Sobibor at Hagen, by prosecutor Schermer.

[20]Carlo Schipper, *La Risiera,* Trieste: Associazone della Resistenza, 1961. Our inquiry in Trieste, March 1970, was published in the Bolletino della Communita Israelitica di Milano.

[21]Novitch, *The Truth about Treblinka,* Presses du temps present, 1967.

[22]M. Novitch, *"The Extermination of Gypsies,"* Paris: A.M.I.F., 1969.

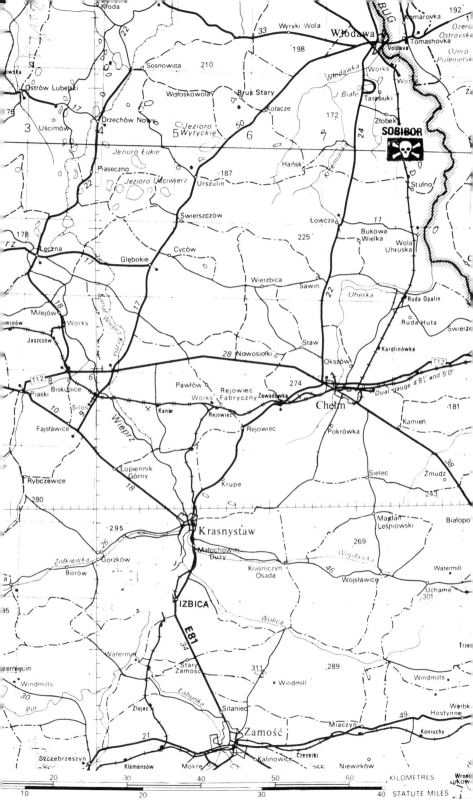

Based on a draft by SS man Erich Bauer who testified as witness at the Hagen trial of 1964.

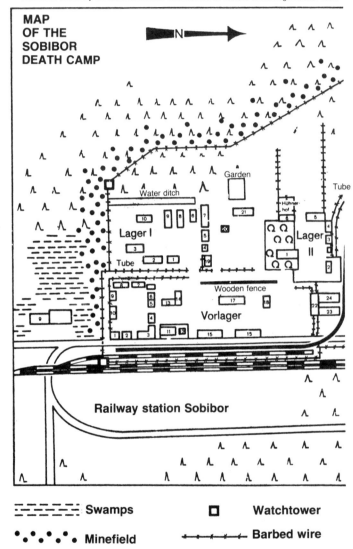

MAP
OF THE
SOBIBOR
DEATH CAMP

N →

Garden

Water ditch

Tube

Hühner-hof

Lager I

Lager II

Tube

Wooden fence

Vorlager

Railway station Sobibor

Swamps ▫ Watchtower

Minefield Barbed wire

VORLAGER: 1. Guard, 2. Dentist and arrest bunker for the Ukrainians, 3. SS kitchen, 4. Garage, 5. Old stables and barber, 6. SS bathroom, 7. SS laundry, 8. Living quarters of the camp leadership, 9. Office of Wagner, Gomerski, etc., 10. SS clothing store. 11. Former post office, 12. Armory, 13. thru 18. Ukrainian barracks, 19. Bakery, 20. SS ironing room, 21. Jewish shoe storage, 22. Transitory barrack, 23. and 24. Jewish luggage storage, 25. Sorting barrack, 26. and 27. Clothing storage, 28. Haircutting of Jewish women.

LAGER I: 1. Tailor Shop, 2. Cobblers and saddlers shop, 3. Carpentry and smithery, 4. Cobblers for Ukrainians, 5. Tool storage, 6. Kitchen, 7. Barrack for Jewish women, 8. & 9. Barracks for Jewish men, 10. Painting shop.

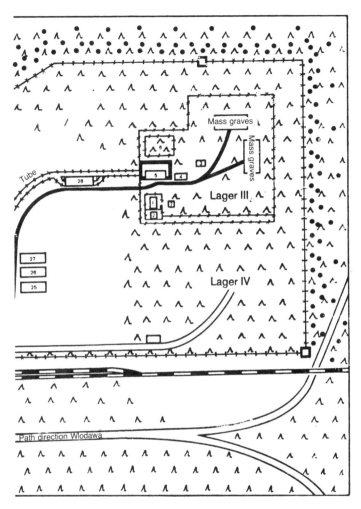

| A A A A Evergreen forest | ▭▬▭▬▭ Railroad |
| Ω Ω Ω Ω Deciduous forest | ▬▬▬▬ Narrow gauge line with dump cars |

LAGER II: 1. Office and SS bedrooms. Storage of valuables, 2. Provisions brought by deportees, 3. Scale, 4. Storage of silverware, 5. Stable and cowshed, 6. Pigsty and chicken coop.

LAGER III: 1. Jewish barrack, 2. Kitchen; dentist, 3. SS blockhouse, 4. Machine shop, 5. Gas chamber, 6. Fenced enclosure, 7. Watchtower with reflectors.

LAGER IV: Has not been completed. Was supposed to store and repair captured Russian weapons.

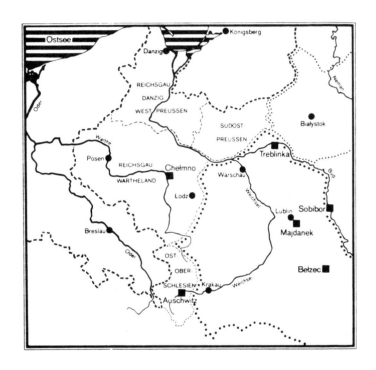

Ostsee

Königsberg

Danzig

REICHSGAU
DANZIG
WEST PREUSSEN

SUDOST
PREUSSEN

Białystok

Warthe

Posen

REICHSGAU

Chełmno

Treblinka

WARTHELAND

Warschau

Lodz

Lublin

Sobibor

Majdanek

Breslau

Oder

OST

OBER

SCHLESIEN Krakau

Weichsel

Bełzec

Auschwitz

Weichsel

FROM IZBICA TO SOBIBOR

TESTIMONY OF TOMASZ BLATT

In front of me stood a man who was still young, his thin face showing apprehension. He feared that his story was boring, that I had no time to listen to him. Several times I had to reassure him.

The Beginning of the War

I lived in Izbica, a large market town in the region of Lublin. I remember the proclamations in the market place calling for general mobilization, and the town clerk explaining the elementary rules of air raid defense procedures. Streets emptied when he came through, and the inhabitants returned home in order to stick paper on their windows. On the same day we had the first air-raid alert and the neighboring village was bombed. In the evening, we learned that a military convoy had arrived at our railway station. The Jewish population collected food parcels for soldiers. Two days later, Izbica was bombed. Although material damage was not very serious, my family decided to leave for the village of Panska-Dolina where a Polish regiment was stationed. After the retreat, Jewish families wondered if they should remain there or escape to Russia. The older generation, remembering the First World War, advised us to remain; the younger ones preferred to run to the East. Others, like my family, returned to Izbica.

Arriving there, we learned that the Germans were there, but that they were ready to leave. Curious to see a German soldier, I ran out and, near a bakery, I saw one putting bread into a bag. I stopped in front of him, and he said: "Guten Tag." He looked quite pleasant and I was amazed. Then I watched the arrival of the Russians. A communist delegation was formed to greet them. What was peculiar about the Red Army was that they all wore the same uniform, and nobody could tell the difference between ordinary soldiers and officers. Their troops requisitioned nothing and remained only a short time. When they left, a crowd of refugees followed them.

I saw my mother crying and trying to convince my father to leave with the Russians. "Let us go with the children; I speak Russian and we shall manage." My father refused. "Germans are not so bad; a refugee's life is humiliating," he answered.

With the first presence of the Germans in Izbica, six Jews were killed, but we believed that they were only war casualties, and not victims of anti-Semitism. However, we became anxious when local Nazis attacked some Jews with hand grenades, injuring many and killing a woman.

When the Germans occupied Lublin, they placed a Kommandantur in Krasnystaw, a small nearby town.

Because of our fear of the local Nazis, Maria Roetenstein, speaking in the name of the population, asked the Germans to maintain order. A Kommandantur was created in Izbica. At the same time, a man named Jan Schultz, pretending to be a refugee from Poznan, opened a watchmaker's shop. In fact, he was a Nazi spy. Soon after his arrival, armed police, in the presence of Schultz, arrested my father and other Jewish notables, and ordered them to form a Jewish council.

We kept receiving bad news from Lublin: Jews were compelled to wear a badge with the star of David, and there were also rumors of torture inflicted by the Gestapo.

Labor Camps

Two labor camps were built in our district, one in Mokre, near Zamosc, the other in Janow-Lubelski. Working conditions were dreadful. At first, laborers were allowed to return home in the evening, but, later, they had to remain in the camps. The task of the Jewish council was to choose those who were to work in camps. Initially, it decided to send the poor and the unemployed.

When Poznan became integrated into the Reich, its Jewish population was deported to the district of Lublin. A thousand natives of Kolo arrived in Izbica, each with only twenty kilos of luggage that they had been allowed to take. The Kominkowski and Frenkel families became our lodgers.

Ukrainians and Germans spread terror everywhere. I was working as a mechanic at the Volksdeutsch Plate shop. Collaborators wore a blue uniform and an armband with the inscription "General Government," and on their helmets one could see an emblem representing a deer. They were armed with revolvers and truncheons and were nicknamed the "Blues."

The Police and the SS were beginning to shoot Jews for fun, and that is how my friend, Leizer, was murdered. New people from Kolo and Konin were deported to our town and we took in the Kohn family. 400 refugees lived in the synagogue. After June 22, 1941 and the assault on Russia, we built a hiding-place in the attic.

Chelmno, the First Death Camp

Mr. Kohn, our lodger from Kolo, got a message from his son, saying that in Chelmno, in the Poznan district, people were gassed. Nobody believed him.

The Gestapo was stationed in Izbica. Two SS men, Engel and Ludwig Klein, with Schultz's help, plundered the ghetto. One evening, Engel, Klein and Schultz arrived at our house with a soldier. We stood against the wall while they broke doors, opening cupboards and taking what they fancied. They tossed around whatever was left and took my father away. Then Schultz came back; the SS had left their gloves. Outside, Engel ordered my father to run, then shot at him but did not hit him.

I remember Engel killing thirty-five people, among them children; my young friend, Peretz Dorfman, thirteen years old, was murdered on the staircase.

Following the Poznan Jews, German Jews came to Izbica. Overcrowding and distress became unbearable and an epidemic of typhus carried off my little brother.

A new law forbade Jews, under the threat of death, to possess furs. We sold ours to Poles, refusing to give them to the Germans. The Gestapo confiscated them and imposed a heavy fine.

Anti-Jewish Acts

One night we were awakened by shooting. People were being chased to the market place. My family and our lodgers went to our hiding place in the attic. I pushed a wardrobe against the entrance and locked it, then hid under the staircase. The following morning, we learned that a cattle train had taken to the East those people who were caught that night.

We forced ourselves to believe that trains took the refugees to labor camps; we hoped the German regime would soon change, and that the end of the war was imminent. Sceptics said that this information came from the "I.W.A. Agency" *("Idn willen azoi"),* meaning "Jews want it so."

Two days after the departure of the convoy, rumors spread that trains were leaving for Belzec, a death factory. We still refused to believe it.

Convoys from Czechoslovakia

Soon, hiding places became useless, although some were arranged as real bunkers and could hold more than a hundred people.

Some people were deported to the East, while others arrived from there. Soon we had in Izbica more Jews from Czechoslovakia than from Poland.

One day, a man entered our workshop, cleanly dressed but very pale. "I have a jacket to sell, do you know a buyer?" he said. I asked my landlady, but she refused. The man left and fainted at the door. I ran towards him. "I haven't eaten for a week," he told us. My landlady gave him soup and bread. The man could hardly eat and wept like a child.

(Thomas Blatt continued to relate his arrival at Sobibor and his stay in the camp until the preparations for the uprising.)

The Revolt

The participants in the revolt were divided into three groups: first, the commanders, Alexander Pechersky and Leon Feldhendler; second, five prisoners, whose duty would be to execute some Nazis; the third group included thirty people in charge of secondary tasks. I belonged to the last group.

From 4 to 5 o'clock in the afternoon, we had to liquidate most of the SS and take over the arsenal. Then we would carry the arms seized from the Nazis to the carpenters' barracks. At 5 P.M. we were to go to camp No. 1. From there, the general uprising would begin. We were to walk to the entrance gate, and those who spoke Russian would force the Ukrainian guard to join us. In fact, we didn't fear them much, as they were armed only when on duty.

A few men were charged to throw stones at the minefield surrounding the camp, in order to make our escape less dangerous. We also relied on the fact that, in the late afternoon, the SS remained in the mess, and some absences in camp wouldn't awake suspicion.

(At that moment, Blatt's voice changed and he seemed to relive the moment of the uprising.)

The day of the revolt was fixed for October 14. At 4:00 P.M. I waited anxiously at camp   for the men to come and kill the Nazis. I heard whispering, "They are coming." Here stood Kali-Mali (his real name was Chubayev), a Soviet prisoner, an engineer aged thirty-five, accompanied by the Kapo Benyo who was our accomplice. They entered the clothing depot. Some minutes earlier, a young prisoner, Phibs, invited the chief of the depot to collect a leather coat that he had ordered. Wolf entered the workshop, and was given a coat, while two prisoners helped him to put it on. At that moment, Kali-Mali killed him with an axe. Prisoners helped with their knives.

Two other SS were liquidated in the same barrack. Drescher went from one group to another to keep us informed. We learned that Niemann, the second-in-command, Greischutz, the leader of the Ukrainian guard, and Klat, were all dead.

Soon the kapos assembled the workers on their way to camp No. 1. Many of the prisoners were still unaware of the events. I ran to the blacksmith's barrack where Shlomo Szmajzner of Pulawy was expecting me. He had a rifle and knew how to use it. He informed me that a *Volksdeutsch* had been killed with an axe near the Ukrainians' camp. We joined the Kapo Benyo and, while the Ukrainians were still quiet, a hurrah was heard from the prisoners. A guard arrived on his bicycle and he was immediately thrown on the ground and knocked down. A prisoner cut his holster and took his revolver. While we were walking towards the main gate, the German cook shot at us, and Shlomo killed him. One of us cut the barbed wire. Many of us didn't wait; they jumped and hit the mines. I was caught in the wires and fell into the ditch. I managed to take off my coat, got out of the ditch and started running. I fell several times, but was not hurt. In the forest, I met Samuel Weitzen of Chodorow, and Freddy Kostman of Cracow. We walked together for hours, tortured with hunger.

In the Forest

In the forest we met many fugitives, and we told each other the success of the Revolt. We were only sorry that SS Frenzl had escaped.

In order not to be recaptured by the Germans, we split into small groups. Our group had only one rifle. I stayed with Weitzen and Freddy Kostman. We reached a house where we saw a comfortable big room occupied by a cat. We asked for some bread from the landlady, who gave us a few slices and a jug of milk, saying, "Do you come from the camp where people are burned? They are looking for you. Run, our village is only five kilometers from there."

We were forced to leave and, in order to attract less attention, we took the road leading to Chelm. I knew the region well and we arrived in Krasnystaw, a heavily populated Jewish village. Alas, all the Jews had already been deported to Sobibor.

In the evening I knocked at the door of a peasant who knew my family and begged him to hide us for a short time, offering him a reward. He put us in his stable and we slept on the straw. Once a day, he brought us a thick soup and bread. We were very hungry, and one day we wanted to leave. He answered, "They will know I have hidden you, and it is a great risk." Indeed, Poles were shot for hiding Jews. We remained in our dark hiding place; we knew it was day when the cock crowed, and when we heard the peasant's steps we knew that night had come.

One day, we heard voices. My companion climbed on a plank and saw a rifle. We heard shots, and I felt a pain in my leg; then a voice said: "Tomorrow we shall bury the Jews." Weitzen was also slightly hurt and Kostman was killed. The attackers left; perhaps they didn't want to use more bullets, maybe they were drunk. We said farewell to our poor companion, kissed him and stepped outside. We ran all night and at dawn we hid in the kiln of an abandoned brick factory. We lived there a long time, going out only at night to search for food.

FROM OPOLE TO SOBIBOR
TESTIMONY OF STANISLAW SZMAJZNER

On May 12, 1942, a cattle truck brought us from Opole to Sobibor. My brother, my cousin and I were jewellers by profession.
On our arrival, we discovered that the SS were looking for craftsmen. Wagner divided the crowds, men on one side, women and
children on the other. From among the former, he selected fifteen
people.

Although I knew nothing of the horrors in the camp, I felt that
my life was hanging on a thread. I left the ranks and offered my
services, "I am a jeweller and you need me." Wagner looked at me
and was not convinced. My instinct of preservation made me open
my wallet on which was a golden monogram. "Look," I said, "this
is my work." Wagner examined the wallet, and took me away
from the crowd. I took my brother and my cousin along with me.
They were to die, later, in the camp.

The SS led our small group inside the camp, and the remaining people went to the gas chambers. We were put into a hut
and given ersatz coffee and a tin of sardines.

Commander Stangl

The next day, we had our first contact with the camp commander. Always smiling, he seemed at ease in Sobibor. He ordered me to make for him a silver ring, engraved with the sym-
bols of life and death. I understood that life was for him and his
guards and that death was for us, the Jewish prisoners. Stangl

himself didn't do any killings. Always sitting in his office, he was the accountant of death. I made rings for him and his assistant, Gustav Wagner. As they seemed pleased with my work, I asked them for news about my parents. Wagner answered gently, "They are well, and be sure that you will join them soon." On May 18, I received a message from a deported friend: "Say kaddish for your parents, they are dead with all the others." From that day on, I sought only revenge.

All the SS were jealous of the commander's rings and forced me to make some for them. They wanted gold rings. Gold was not scarce, but the SS had no right to take it, as it belonged to the state. Therefore, they forced the prisoners to steal jewelry and gold from camp No. 3. I made a small furnace to melt the rings and secretly produced thirty-two of them. Stangl and Wagner soon learned that other SS had rings. Wagner, mad with fury, caught me and dragged me to camp No. 3. Feeling that my last hour had come, I begged him, "Master of life and death, you saved me once, spare me again." He liked my pathos and forgave me.

Family Life

All officers, non-coms and ordinary soldiers were often away on leave. For every three months of work they got three weeks of vacation. They took home suitcases full of clothes that had been manufactured by the prisoners, shoes, eau-de-Cologne, luxury items stolen from French or Dutch prisoners, poultry and ham. They also ordered me to melt gold, and for some I even made gold soles for their shoes.

Like Wounded Birds

I remember one particularly dreadful event; it was the arrival of a convoy from Majdanek. I don't know how many prisoners were there; skinny, clothed in striped pajamas, they were led brutally to camp No. 2. The gas chambers were out of action that day, and the wretched people spent the night in the open, lying on the ground, awaiting death. Their voices were not human, but resembled the wailing of injured animals; it was awful to listen to them. What is more, the SS didn't sleep either. They got up in the middle of the night to beat up their victims with sticks and whips. After their execution, their screams still seemed to float in the air, like the cry of wounded birds.

October 14 is an important day in the history of the Holocaust: 600 unarmed prisoners grabbed arms and overcame 40 SS men and 200 Ukrainians.

In the preparations for the uprising, my job was stealing weapons. As I was in charge of repairing the stoves of the Ukrainian barracks, I stole many rifles and hid them safely. These rifles enabled us to kill more than twenty soldiers. I took a rifle into the forest.

Our life and struggle in the Polish forest is a different story; we needed loads of imagination and courage to survive.

FROM LUBLIN TO SOBIBOR

TESTIMONY OF HELLA FELLENBAUM-WEISS

Deportations in Lublin began in 1939. I was fourteen years old, and one of a family of four children.

At first, nobody was sent to the gas chambers, but to the village of Siedliszcze. My mother managed to take with her some clothing, jewels and silver. We survived by selling these possessions. We lived in a hut, and were put to work (even the children) by German order. We were promised wages and food, but never received any. We had to dig irrigation canals and plough the ground.

Later, my parents were sent to Wlodawa, forty kilometers away; children went to Staw, an infernal camp. We had to work outdoors, scantily dressed and barefooted. Then we were transferred to Wlodawa where we hoped to find our parents, but, in November, 1942, a massive deportation had taken place from Wlodawa to Sobibor and my parents were already dead. We were not aware that we were going to follow them.

We left for Sobibor in carts. One might wonder why so few of us tried to escape, since we knew the fate awaiting us. True, my brothers and I were still children, but why didn't the adults revolt? Our cart was guarded by an armed Ukrainian who was watching us. German soldiers with machine guns rode alongside us on horseback. At the border of a wood, my young brother gave a farewell sign, left the cart and started to run, followed by my older brother. My little brother fell; the other escaped. I learned later that he, too, was murdered.

I am confused about the time of our arrival at Sobibor; I only remember that we crossed a forest and then I saw an inscription on a poster: "Sonderkommando Sobibor." As in a dream, I heard a German ask: "Who can knit?" I stepped forward. The German asked me to leave the crowd and took me to a barrack with two other girls.

My mother had taught me how to knit socks. I knitted for the SS and the Ukrainians; I also ironed shirts. Carpenters made me a stool on which I stood when the SS came to visit us; it was vital that I should look taller and older than my age.

The Things I Saw

One day, a convoy brought to the camp prisoners in striped pyjamas. They were extremely thin, and their heads were shaved; women and men looked alike and they could hardly walk. Rumors spread that these people, about 300 of them, came from Majdanek where the gas chambers were out of order. When they alighted from the train, they literally collapsed. SS Frenzel met them and poured chloride on their heads, as though they were already dead.

The arrival of another convoy distressed me in the same way. It was thought to come from Lvov, but nobody knew for sure. Prisoners were sobbing and told us a dreadful tale: they had been gassed on the way with chlorine, but some survived. The bodies of the dead were green and their skin had peeled off.

On another day, prisoners arrived from Belzec and were shot immediately. In their pockets we found notes in Yiddish: "We are told we are on our way to work. It is a lie. Avenge us." Later, when I joined the partisans after my escape and was fighting in Poland, in Germany and in Czechoslovakia, I remembered these words. They gave me courage to survive.

Uprising and Escape

We all knew that something was going to happen, but I took no part in the organization of the revolt, or in the execution of its plan. I believe the plan was extremely well conceived, and the leaders had great courage. Many SS were killed, and if only a few of us survived, it was not the fault of the plan but of the general conditions in occupied Poland at that time.

In the Forest

Surviving in the forest was not easy. While running all night, I met two other prisoners; we went on running, not knowing where. Deep in the forest, we found an abandoned hut; inside was a sack of potatoes, a real treasure for us. At night we lit a fire to bake them, and we slept in the attic. However, we couldn't remain in that house for long. One morning we heard German voices; the hut was being searched and we expected to be caught, but the Germans left. As we thought that they would come back, we escaped in the cold and the rain.

Sometimes we approached villages to steal potatoes, or old sacks in order to cover ourselves. One night we saw three lights in the forest; we approached, and heard these words: *"Halt, stehen bleiben"* (Stop!). Three men came near, and we noticed that their "guns" were only shovels! They laughed; apparently, they had mistaken us for robbers. So, to frighten us, they pretended to be Germans. They were, themselves, escaped Russian prisoners. They were a godsend to us. They were clever, knowing no fear. Using their shovels as guns, they regularly managed to steal enough food for all of us. One day, they brought us a pig.

We were looking for partisans, and eventually found them. I joined the regiment of Prokopyuk. During later battles, I won a medal for courage, a Red Star medal and five commendations: the first, on October 18, 1944; the second, November 2, after the battles of Michalowce and Tymen; one on January 20, 1945, when Persow and Kosice were captured; and, lastly, for the capture of Morawska-Ostrava on May 8, 1945.

In Czechoslovakia, I met a young Jew in General Swoboda's army. We married and left for Israel. We have three daughters.

FROM MIELEC TO SOBIBOR
TESTIMONY OF EDA LICHTMAN

On September 5, 1939, Wieliczka was occupied by the Wehrmacht. In the first week, the soldiers killed dogs and cats. On September 11, the first round-up of Jews took place: they were forced to collect garbage from the market place. Those who worked slowly were hit with bayonets. The next day thirty-two Jews were arrested and were piled into a lorry that was leaving for the woods. They were followed by vehicles full of German officers and soldiers.

We ran after the convoy and, after losing sight of it, followed the tracks of the wheels. We met the soldiers on their way back; passing us, they grinned. Peasants told us: "Don't go any further, you will be killed like the others." In a clearing lay the bodies of the thirty-two men, together with those of four Polish officers, two priests and a highschool teacher. Only Henia's brother, a boy of fourteen, survived.

We brought back the bodies, and buried them in the Jewish cemetery of our village. The murderers had ripped off their clothes and wedding rings.

As the occupying forces requisitioned Jewish houses, I left with my husband for Mielec. There, too, the Jewish community was condemned to forced labor, and many executions took place. In the streets, we wore the badge with the star of David. I remember a mad-looking German aviator who hit every Jew that he met with his cane. I also remember that Jews were locked up in the synagogue which was set on fire, with soldiers making sure that nobody escaped.

In the ghetto, distress and hunger overcame us. The authorities promised not to deport us if we paid them a ransom. Everyone brought his possessions: jewels, crystal-ware, even wool and coffee. After a quiet night, we were awakened by shots; an entire division had surrounded the ghetto. Armed *Feldgraus* and Ukrainians entered our houses: *"Raus, raus! Alle raus!"* (Everybody out). Some of us were still undressed, others hurriedly gathered bags, suitcases and parcels.

We were collected in the market place where the elderly and invalids were killed on the spot. Eight hundred survivors were sent to an unknown destination. Poles were watching us, some crossing themselves and whispering, "Today it is you, tomorrow us." Others sneered. Snow was falling heavily.

In our convoy, a new-born baby was crying in its mother's arms. She had no milk, so she gathered some snow, put it into a feeding bottle and warmed it in her breast before giving it to the child.

We stopped in Berdychow, and were taken to a hangar where we were locked up. Bread was put on tables and soldiers ordered us to eat. When we approached the tables, the Germans started to shoot and laughed at us. We remained hungry.

The next morning there was a new selection. At the entrance to the hangar, the Nazis had placed a wooden case that looked like a radio set, and we were told that it was to test our physical strength. Some of us were told to return to the hangar, others to remain outside. These orders were punctuated by blows of whips and revolvers. The judge of Mielec, Pohoryles, asked in German, "Who are you? Mind your own business." Pohoryles snatched the whip from a German, but was thrown on the ground and murdered, together with his wife and son.

We spent a few days in Berdychow to bury our dead. Then we were led to the station, forced to undress in the snow and lie in empty wagons.

Young naked girls, crying with rage and shame, were forced to dance for the SS. A new selection began and more convoys were formed: some for Biala-Podlaska, some for Miedzyrzec, others for Dubienka on the river Bug. When I boarded the last train, I was a widow.

From Dubienka to Sobibor

At Dubienka, we were lodged in synagogues where the Jewish community gave us food and straw. Some days later we were housed with families, and were compelled to work on Aryan properties. A group of Jews wearing their prayer shawls were led towards a hill, and told to tread and dance on holy books. Nobody returned alive.

Many high officers, accompanied by Ukrainian volunteers (nicknamed the *Pizaki* or Black ones), often visited the ghetto in order to steal from us. They always left behind a trail of wounded and dead. I remember one of these visits when some families were assembled, and an SS officer threw a hand grenade. I still see these murdered children bathed in their own blood.

We were not only massacred for pleasure. The propaganda machine of the Wehrmacht, wanting to film the destruction of a partisan camp, forced young Jews to play the parts of Resistance fighters. The camera took pictures of the valiant German army. However, the bullets were real . . .

We received orders to leave for Hrubieszow. People fell dead on the journey; little children begged, "Sir, please kill me, but spare papa!"

Hrubieszow was a camp surrounded by barbed wire and watchtowers with armed guards. We left the train in silence, and guards were shooting to keep us even quieter.

At night, the ghetto residents were allowed to bring us bread and water. At dawn, we were taken to a cattle train and told, "You are leaving for the Ukraine." We were very thirsty, but the doors opened only to allow Ukrainian guards, dressed in German uniforms, to steal our last belongings. These sadists cut the fingers of some of us in order to snatch rings.

We lost all notion of time when the train stopped. Blinded by the sun, I could read: *SS Sonderkommando Sobibor.*

Sobibor

Officers and soldiers with machine guns were waiting for us. One of them held a big dog on a leash. An officer called me, "You, there, what is your profession?" I replied, "Kindergarten teacher." The Nazi roared with laughter. "Well, here you will wash our laundry." I left the ranks with two young women, Bella Sobol and Serka Katz from Dubienka, and we were led into the camp to a little barrack. Some clothing was lying around, proof that other people had been there before. What had happened to them? Out of 7,000 people who left Hrubieszow, only three women remained alive in Sobibor. Of these three, I am the only survivor.

Everyday Life in Sobibor

On our arrival, two prisoners, watched by a guard, brought us two trunks of dirty linen to be washed in two days, after it had been disinfected.

I remember that first night. I heard screams, and opened the door, but received lashes of a whip across my face. *Oberwachmann* Lachmann, who was taking his dog for a walk, shouted, "If I see you here again, I shall send you Barry (the dog)." Later I learned that these screams came from young girls who were raped before being gassed.

From our barrack, I could hear people begging for water. From time to time, a prisoner was allowed to go to the well where the *Volksdeutsch* Michel was waiting. With his bayonet, he pushed the wretched victim to the latrines. "Gather your excrement with your bare hands!" he screamed. Then he led the prisoner to the guard, Malinowski, who shot him.

There were other games. Michel enjoyed the sight of a young boy, Szymon, pushing a wheelbarrow full of sand until he fell exhausted to the ground. Szymon took part in the revolt, but died while escaping.

One day, not seeing any soldier, I carried a bucket of water to a group of inmates. Suddenly I felt a blow and heard SS man Fritz Rewald shouting, "You are lucky I am alone, but if I see you again . . ." It was strictly forbidden to approach newcomers.

I also remember two prisoners carrying a stretcher with a young woman in labor. After a few minutes, we heard the wailing of a new-born child. SS Wagner was present, and ordered the Ukrainian guard to throw the baby into the latrines. The mother was taken to camp No. 3. Some days later, the body of the new-born was floating in the ditch, amidst the excrement.

Another time, in a convoy from Vienna, the SS selected three beautiful singers, who were forced to perform until the Nazis became tired. Then the girls were executed.

From a convoy of Berlin prisoners, three girls, aged sixteen or seventeen, were spared, and Ruth became Paul Groth's favorite. Later, all three were murdered.

Prisoners from western Europe were better dressed and seemed less hungry than Polish Jews. They had rucksacks and nice suitcases. Many of them were selected for labor camps in Lublin, Sawnin, Krychow and Ossowa. Some months later, exhausted, they were sent to the gas chambers.

The Camp Guards

Karl Frenzel, Gustav Wagner, Hermann Michel, Goetzinger, Otto Weiss, Bredow, Steubel, Paul Groth and Hubert Gomerski lived in a villa called *Schwalbennest* (Swallows' nest). Karl Muller, Richter, John Kliehr, Nowak, the two Wolf brothers, Boscher, Greischutz, Schuett, Falanster, Unverhau, Erich Bauer, named their villa *Am lustigen Floh* (the happy flea).

Each SS officer had his own way of killing. They were all waiting for the arrival of the convoys. Bredow was on the lookout for very young girls whom he used to whip sadistically. Gomerski killed the prisoners with a truncheon that had nails in it; Groth and Bolender came with their dog. When they said to a deportee, *"Ah, du willst nicht arbeiten?"* (Ah, you refuse to work?) the dog tore the victim to pieces. The camp commander wore a cloak and white gloves. He described the happiness awaiting those who left for the Ukraine. "Life conditions and food are much better there than here . . . Certificates will be given to good workers, families will be united." We were not allowed to express the slightest doubt.

SS *Scharführer* Erich Bauer, master of camp No. 3, supervised the executions from a roof window of the gas chambers. Short and stocky, always drunk, he threatened to hang us by the feet. He was never seen without his machine gun. I recall his visit to the laundry on a Saturday. "Ah! you are working on Saturday; you must be communists." A prisoner from Sochaczew answered that he was a practising Jew but was forced to work. Bauer addressed the woman, Saba Salz, "And do you also work on Saturday?" The Sochaczew prisoner answered for her, "Our women don't pray; they light Sabbath candles on Friday evening." Bauer asked, "Do you light candles here?" "I did it at home," said the woman. Bauer replied, "I hate religious Jews; they are all dirty."

In Bauer's room, there was a photograph of himself with his family, together with the Führer. He had a private bar, and once a month we made liquors for him with egg yolks. One day, he broke a bottle; Berek Brand, a prisoner, had to clean the floor with his tongue; the man's face was cut with glass.

One day, Paul Groth ordered four prisoners to carry him around the camp, while he was seated in an armchair. He amused himself by throwing burning pieces of paper on the victims.

Shaul Stark looked after geese; he fed them and weighed them every day. Once, a goose became ill and died. Frenzel, Bredow, Wagner and Weiss whipped Stark to death. The man's last words were: "Avenge me, comrades, avenge me."

We were always hungry. Frenzel, having caught a child of thirteen stealing a tin of sardines, ordered all prisoners to form a circle around the boy. Then he murdered him with these words, "This is the fate awaiting thieves."

The Nazis selected some painters to decorate their rooms; they had a preference for landscapes, which they sent to their families. They also seemed to enjoy gymnastic sessions that were imposed on the prisoners: we had to run, jump, climb. While running, we were beaten up. These sessions took place once a day, but after some of us tried to escape, they were increased to morning and evening.

Karl Mueller had refined tastes and wanted his clothes washed and ironed every morning. I used to bring them to him, and was accompanied by Esther Gruenberg and Saba Salz. Every time, he asked us the same question and gave himself the same answer, "What is the fiercest animal in the world? Don't you know it? It is man."

Games in Sobibor

One evening, SS officer Otto Weiss prepared a coffin in which a prisoner, dressed as a hassid was laid out. Together with other

Nazis, Weiss sang: *"Ich bin ein Jude mit einer langen Nase!"* (I am a Jew with a long nose). Then the prisoner got up, saluted, and repeated the song. Weiss continued singing:

Gott du unser lieber
Erhöre unsere Lieder,
Mach dem Juden die Klappe zu,
Dann haben die Menschen Ruh. Amen.

(God, listen to our song, and put an end to the Jews; people then will enjoy peace).

We had to punctuate the song with "Amen, Amen!"

Once, Wagner ordered a prisoner to sing. He was very dark and had been nicknamed "der Neger" (the negro). He improvised verses in Yiddish:

Wie lustig ist da unser Leben
Man tut uns zu essen geben.
Wie lustig ist im grünen Wald,
Wo ich mich aufhalt.

(Our life is happy here, we receive good food; how happy we are in the green forest where I stay).

Wagner enjoyed the song so much that he forced us to repeat it every evening. The "negro," a cobbler, had lost his wife and two children. We became great friends. I remember that on the night of October 13, while we were making the last preparations for the revolt, he said to me, "Let us swear that we shall fight, and the young ones will know freedom." Then he knelt and kissed the ground while we were overcome with emotion.

The "negro" was part of the group to attack the arms depot. He was killed by Volksdeutscher Schreiber while passing arms to the rebels. The same day, Schreiber was killed by Shaul Fleishhacker of Kalisz.

Shaul was a courageous man. Once, Wagner had ordered him to whip a young prisoner twenty-five times for stealing some butter; Shaul refused to obey, and received twenty-five lashes.

Shaul had a wife and three sons in Kalisz, and hoped he would find them one day.

Himmler's Visit

At the end of winter, 1943, our guards became very excited: the *Reichsführer* Himmler was coming to Sobibor.

A special airport was improvised opposite the depot. On the day of the visit, all prisoners were locked in the barracks. The commander of the camp and his officers received Himmler and his staff. After having toured camps 1 and 2, they reached camp 3 where they watched an execution of young people. The same day, a great banquet was given in honor of the visit. I was asked to bring flowers to decorate the tables. Himmler was delighted with his visit. When he left, our executioners wore new decorations.

The Camp and the Outside World

Since there were some attempts to escape, new soldiers were brought in, mines were laid around the camp, and the barbed wire was electrified. Gustav Wagner supervised the work. One day, Rywka, a girl of thirteen, was given twenty-five lashes for falling asleep while digging a ditch. Another day, Nazis escorting a convoy asked to visit the camp. The guards refused. A few days later they returned with a special authorization, and were treated to a dinner in the mess. Wagner, Niemann and Schwartz showed them how the prisoners worked, and they were given stolen objects from the inmates: perfume, cosmetics, jewelry.

There were all kinds of things in store: clothes, furs, surgical instruments, shoes. A special room contained gold and jewels; gold coins, bracelets, brooches, were sorted out in different compartments by a naked prisoner, under the supervision of SS man Steubel. A German jeweller came regularly to the camp to make an inventory of the booty which was then sent to Berlin.

Before the camp was surrounded by minefields, two prisoners managed to dig the earth beneath the barbed wire and escaped. The next day, one prisoner out of ten was condemned to twenty-five lashes; while being beaten, he had to count out loud the number of lashes that he received. If he made an error, the SS started beating him again. Some of us got up to 100 lashes. Finally the hostages were led to camp No. 3 and executed. A young singer who wanted to share her friend's fate ran after him, insulting the SS.

Tortures Inflicted on Young Prisoners

There was a model stable in the camp and a thirteen year-old prisoner, Max, was in charge. Once, Frenzel, unhappy with the boy's work, started to beat him up, and soon was helped by Becker, Nowak, Groth and Klat. Max lost consciousness and, from that day on, he couldn't face a German without trembling. He screamed every night, and soon afterwards was murdered.

Karl Frenzel had noticed that Leibl Fleischer, aged thirteen, was stammering. "What is your name?," he often asked, and "What have you eaten to-day, dirty dog?" The SS enjoyed that little game so much that he rewarded the boy with a hard egg and a sandwich. Fleischer was to fall in the uprising.

The Heroism of the Young Prisoners

Berek Lichtman, who came to Sobibor with his whole family, was the only survivor. Though he was only fifteen, he was always quiet and serene. He first worked in the laundry, then in the kitchen, and finally in the shoemakers' barracks. During the revolt, when SS Falaster was killed, Berek kept his calm, helped to hide the body and clean the traces of blood. He fell during the revolt, while shooting at the guards to cover the prisoners' escape.

Solidarity among the Prisoners

Many prisoners caught typhus, but tried to go to work for fear of being murdered, as the Nazis killed the sick. Simon Rabinowicz found a little kerosene stove and cooked some rice, saving the life of many sick people. Once he was caught carrying food to a patient, and was beaten up by Otto Weiss. In spite of it, he continued his work. Another day, Frenzel entered the barracks at the same time when Simon was cooking. The poor man hid the saucepan under his foot; I remember how much he suffered from the burns that he got. He took an important part in the revolt, and was killed while escaping.

One day, the Ukrainian Koszewadski brought the white uniform of his chief, *Oberwachmann* Lachmann, and ordered me to have it ready by 5 o'clock the next day. "But it won't be ready!" I said. To answer a guard! The Ukrainian began to hit me, when the prisoner Itzhak caught his hand. "Aren't you ashamed to hit a woman who is working so hard?" Koszewadski left the barrack; he never hit a woman again.

In camp No. 1, there was a dispensary that was visible from the train station and that was reserved only for the Germans. Dr. Bressler from Plock, and his two assistants, Kurt and Bertha, deportees from Czechoslovakia, were in charge of the dental section. They often risked their lives to smuggle medicines to us, and gave us treatment.

From the window of the laundry, I once saw a group of prisoners being led to camp 3, the gas chambers and crematoria. A little boy was too slow in following the group. A dog approached him, but didn't harm him. A guard took the child by the hand and made him join the cortege of death.

During the winter, convoys often carried children who were frozen to death. SS Wagner, a cigarette in his mouth, piled up the little bodies. From time to time, one could hear a scream. The children were not all dead . . .

FROM WARSAW TO SOBIBOR
TESTIMONY OF ABRAHAM MARGULIES

I was born in Zyrardow in 1921, and lived in Warsaw when the War broke out. My mother believed there would be less danger in a small town and took us to Zamosc. There we were arrested and my brother and I were sent to a labor camp in Janowice.

In May, 1941, attempting to avoid deportation, we both hid, but were denounced and sent to the train station. Three thousand people from Zamosc and Izbica were waiting on the platform. "Where are we going?" we kept asking. "Is it to Belzec, the death camp?" We knew nothing when we boarded the train, but we soon realized that we were not going to Belzec, but eastwards; the journey was short, and two SS men, Gustav Wagner and Hubert Gomerski, were waiting on the platform, shouting: "Men to the left, women and children to the right." Then Wagner selected about fifty men, including me. An hour later, a Ukrainian guard brought us bread, butter and jam. I asked, "Where are the women and children?" The guard answered, "Don't worry, they are better treated than you; they are having chocolate."

The Beginning

We couldn't sleep that first night. In the morning I joined a group of twenty prisoners and cleaned the carriages. Each train consisted of thirty or more wagons, and we did the cleaning under the supervision of Paul Groth, who stood with a whip in one hand and a gun in the other. Our group included very young boys, fourteen or fifteen years old. When one of them was tired, Paul Groth told him, "Ah! you feel tired? Go to the hospital." These words meant that the prisoner would get a bullet in his head.

During the first week, I couldn't get used to the idea that the 3,000 deported people were already dead.

Sobibor functioned without stop from May to August 1942. Three or four trains arrived daily. When we were late in our work, the SS man let his dog loose, and Barry (the dog) would run from one prisoner to the other, tearing out pieces of flesh. There were also night convoys.

One day, as a convoy of mentally ill arrived, the Nazis forced them to do physical exercises before sending them to the gas chambers. Another day, when a group came from Biala Podlaska, the SS officer chose fifty people, and told us to put on hats, while the newcomers were to remain bareheaded. All of us were ordered to run, and were beaten while running. On the same day, an old man was hanged on a tree near the platform for refusing to eat jam mixed with sand. Once a convoy arrived from the Janowski camp, near Lvov. There were as many dead as there were living, and the SS gave us cigarettes to hide the stench of the decomposing bodies.

Resistance

Chelm was eight kilometers from Sobibor and its nearest railway station. When the trains were passing nearby, we could hear them. Once, when we cleaned the carriages, we found many dead bodies and learned that there had been an attempt of escape.

When the deportees resisted, the SS did not undress them, but dragged them to the gas chambers.

Strangely, the prisoners from western Europe — Holland, Germany and France — remained calm. Once, a woman asked where the next train was stationed, so that she would be able to continue her journey. I also remember a woman carrying a beautiful, smiling baby. Just thinking of that lovely child ending its life in the crematorium, I began to cry and ran like a madman.

The Kitchens

There were three kitchens in the camp: one for the SS personnel, under Wagner's supervision. He used to select very young girls whom he enjoyed beating up. A second kitchen was for the Ukrainian guards. Krupka, their chief, hated the Germans and often gave us news from the front. He promised to contact the partisans and we gave him some gold to take to them, but the attack on the camp never took place and Krupka disappeared.

Hershel Zuckerman, from Kurow, was in charge of the Jewish kitchen. After the cleaning of the carriages, I was assigned to help in the kitchen, but didn't stay long. I tried to smuggle some food to women who worked in the laundry, and Frenzel caught me and sent me back to the wagons.

An old German, Kliehr, supervised the bakery and was quite humane. At night, he used to bring bread into our camp.[1]

There was a large pig-sty in our camp; the SS took ham with them when on leave to see their families. Fruit and vegetables were also grown, under the care of Shaya of Chelm, Abraham of Izbica and Helka Weiss. The Nazis gave the impression that we lived in a very peaceful place . . .

Camp No. 3

Nobody was allowed to approach that camp. Once, while working in the forest, I noticed a half naked prisoner. "They have burned my father," he was crying.

Himmler and his staff came to Sobibor at the end of February, 1943. Two hundred young women were gassed in their presence.

The Revolt

At first, it was fixed for October 13, but was postponed for a day, because of an unexpected visit of friends of the SS.

Fifteen prisoners were to attack the barracks of the Ukrainian guards, fifteen others were to assault the munitions depot. We were 700 prisoners in Sobibor, including eighty women, and some children.

64

On October 14, I was sent, along with Biskubicz, to do some work at the gate. I saw Niemann on his horse, leaving for the tailors' workshop. There, he was to be killed with an axe. SS Beckmann was sitting at his desk when the rebels entered; he tried to defend himself with a paper-knife, but was stabbed.

Our plan for invading the Ukrainian barracks did not materialize. Bauer, the leader of camp No. 3, arrived earlier than expected; he sat in a lorry full of drinks, and Frenzel called four prisoners to help him to unload them. Suddenly, a group of inmates appeared at the camp entrance where the ground was not mined. The Ukrainians started shooting; Frenzel was standing with his machine gun. I ran towards the barbed wire and, with the help of Helka Weiss, managed to cut it with pliers. I saw Sasha passing me, a revolver in his hand. I heard mines exploding, and saw a Russian prisoner covering our escape with his gun.

At last, we were in the forest, free . . . At dawn, hidden in the wood, I heard Frenzel's voice; he was talking to a peasant, "We shall have them all! A division with tanks is after them; there is a reward of 400 zlotys per head." The peasants saw us, but did not betray us . . .

[1]At his trial in Berlin in 1950, together with SS man Bauer, Kliehr was acquitted because of the testimony in his favor given by survivors Esther Raab and Lerner.

FROM IZBICA TO SOBIBOR
TESTIMONY OF SIMHA BIALOWITZ

In the autumn of 1942, I was a hospital attendant for Dr. Hermann Strauss. One day, there was an SS order: "All personnel must go to the railway station." There, SS man Engel, standing near Mr. Blatt, the president of the Jewish council, was killing people for no reason at all. The staircase was littered with dead bodies.

When I left the station, all the sick people had been murdered. Mad with fright, I ran towards the forest, looking for partisans, but found nobody. However, I remained in the woods, suffering from hunger and cold. When the first snow began to fall I was not alone; I joined a group of more than 300 men. The peasants were saying, "In Izbica, there is a new ghetto; Jews are no longer being deported." We returned to Izbica, as it was impossible to spend the winter in the forest. In Izbica, I found my parents hiding in an old factory. In the new ghetto, among destroyed houses, we were forced to work. "You will remain here until the end of the war," the SS assured us. However, we spent the nights in hiding.

At dawn, on April 28, 1943, we were awakened by shots. I tried to escape, but was caught by the police, beaten up and searched. With 200 people, I was led to the market place, and put into a lorry.

We went first to the camp of Trawniki, near Lublin, but were refused entry. The lorry took us to Sobibor.

Arrival in Sobibor

My thirteen year old brother, Fishel, and my two sisters were arrested the same day as I was. As we got down from the lorry, Gustav Wagner screamed, "Doctors, dentists, pharmacists, plumbers, all forward!" Many answered his appeal, and I dragged my brother with me. The SS chose only five or six people; the others were killed on the spot. Later, a prisoner was to tell me that he saw my two sisters among the victims.

Everything was taken away from us, but I was glad that my young brother was with me. He was sent to the clothing depot, and I was assigned to work in the forest.

Work in the Forest

The Waldkommando consisted of thirty prisoners supervised by SS Mueller and Grimmer, and helped by Ukrainians. We were told: "Work, or you'll get a bullet in your head." It was a rare day when one of us wasn't murdered. The victims were quickly replaced. The work was very hard. The Nazis forced us to sing and organized a new kind of entertainment: a prisoner had to climb to the top of a tree while we were cutting it down. Several of us died, and I was fortunate to escape with only a broken arm. Afterwards, I was sent to work in the pharmacy. The registered pharmacist had been executed and I was replacing him.

The Pharmacy

The prisoners had no right to medicines; these were reserved only for the personnel or were exported. Some deported doctors were in possession of rare medicines. In the pharmacy, one could find toilet soap and eau-de-Cologne. Occasionally, an SS officer arrived, inspected the stock and took some away; they were always looking for morphine.

My job consisted of classifying drugs. Once, when Wagner caught me giving some medicine to prisoners he almost killed me. From time to time, I was sent to camp No. 2. The Nazis took great care of it, as they wanted to hide the horrible truth about Sobibor.

When we passed from one camp to another, we were searched. If something was found on a prisoner, he was shot on the spot.

Plans of Action

We were obsessed with the idea of avenging our dead and killing the SS. Hersh, a young prisoner from Zamosc, suggested poison. He told me: "Try to find three bottles with 200 grams of morphine." I got the morphine and gave it to him, but Wagner found one of the bottles. Four men and one girl were arrested. Wagner showed me the bottle, and I said, "I have never seen it before, our bottles are labeled." The SS officer in charge of the pharmacy confirmed my words. I was lucky, but Hersh and the five others were executed.

I soon learned that the prisoners who worked in the forest were preparing a mass escape. Two men who left with a guard to fetch water and bread, killed him with an axe. When a second guard arrived, the prisoners escaped.

Only the Polish Jews who knew the area and the language could survive after their escape. Ten Dutch prisoners who belonged to the outdoor workers remained behind. Podchlebnik, who killed the guard, and Kopf managed to escape. Later, I learned that Kopf was murdered after the Liberation.

All the other fugitives were recaptured and taken back to camp. Frenzel made a speech about our ignominious behavior, and ten members of the group were executed to avenge the murdered guard.

The Revolt

The committee preparing the revolt consisted of several groups: mine was to find money and valuable objects. My brother and I had a password to enable us to find each other in case we got lost after the escape. During the revolt, I ran from the depot to the barbed wire; I injured my hand, and I still bear the scars. I succeeded in reaching the forest where I found my brother. We ran together, looking for other prisoners. We wandered a long time, hiding in fields.

68

The day after the escape, we were glad to watch the procession of cars carrying the coffins of the murdered Nazis of Sobibor. Alas, very few of us survived the uprising of Sobibor.

FROM PARIS TO SOBIBOR

TESTIMONY OF THE WIDOW OF JOSEPH DUNIETZ

Joseph Dunietz was born in Kiev in 1912. In 1917, his parents settled in Rovno, where Joseph went to high school. Later, he left for France and studied chemistry at the University of Caen. His widow tells us the following:

In 1940, France was occupied. In 1942, at the start of the anti-Jewish persecutions, we were already married, had a little girl, and I was again pregnant. On February 13, 1943, my husband was arrested, sent to Drancy for a month, and then deported to Sobibor. On his way, he tried to escape with other prisoners, but a man from Belgium was caught and shot, and that discouraged the rest of the group.

Over a thousand people travelled in the convoy and, when they reached their destination, ten men were selected, my husband among them. All the others were executed.

In the camp, he did several kinds of work and later played an important role in the revolt. After his escape, he lived in the forest and with peasants. When the war ended, he became the chauffeur of a Polish minister of the first government of the Liberation, in Chelm. Later, he returned to France through Odessa. My husband and I decided to settle in Israel, where he found work. We had two more children. My husband refused to talk about Sobibor, but in 1965, he agreed to testify at the Nazi trial in Hagen. He died of a heart attack at his factory, aged fifty-three, one day before he was to leave for Germany.

FROM SWOLLE TO SOBIBOR

TESTIMONY OF SELMA WIJNBERG

I was born in Swolle, Holland, in 1922. There was no hate between the Jews and the Dutch people; it was only when the Germans occupied the country, that the persecutions began.

In 1941, a camp for German Jews was created in Westerbork. When Jews were forced to wear badges, the Dutch population showed them respect. In 1941, a strike paralyzed Amsterdam for three days in protest against the anti-Jewish measures.[1]

The Dutch people hid the Jews. Therefore, out of a Jewish population of 2,000 in Utrecht, only 200 were deported. A special organization called "Free Holland," helped the Jews by giving them food, money and even evacuating them to England.

In 1942, I was arrested with my family and interned in Westerbork. We were 8,000 prisoners, and the German officers in charge announced that we were going to work in Poland or the Ukraine, and we were to take with us shoes, clothes and food. Letters were arriving from Wlodawa, confirming that life was pleasant in Poland. Later, I knew it was a lie, as the prisoners were forced to sign printed postcards. The name of Sobibor was never mentioned.

Escape from Westerbork

I didn't want to go to Poland, and I ran away from Westerbork. I hid for a long time among Dutch families, but a Volksdeutsche (Dutchman of German origin) denounced me. I spent two months

71

in an Amsterdam prison before being transferred to the camp of Vught, where political prisoners and Jews were interned. There I worked in the laundry.

In March, 1943, we were on our way to Poland. Many of us hoped to meet our families again. Ailing Jews were taken care of during the journey; German nurses distributed medicines to patients.

We reached Sobibor on April 9. The men undressed immediately after leaving the train, then were led to camp No. 3. Women passed through an alley of pine trees, towards a barrack. They took off their clothes and had their hair cut. A German officer chose twenty-eight women to work in camp No. 2.

I spent five months in Sobibor, and it is difficult to imagine the horror of that camp. I remember SS Wolf approaching naked children going to the gas chambers, giving them sweets, and patting their heads. "Keep well, children, everything will be fine," he used to say.

Once, a Dutch prisoner recognized his family's clothes in the depot and saw his wife and children being led to the gas chambers. He wept bitterly and nobody could comfort him. A young man working in camp No. 3 found the body of his father. He took it away for burial, and was killed by the SS.

After the revolt, I managed to escape with two other young girls, Ketty from the Hague, and Ursula Stern from Germany. Ketty joined the partisans and died of typhus. Ursula fought with the partisans. We were together at Westerbork, at Vught and in prison; we were together in Sobibor, and we succeeded in escaping together.[2]

[1]The first deportations of Dutch Jews took place in February, 1941, to the camp of Mauthausen.

[2]This testimony was taken by Ilya Ehrenburg at Chelm, on the 10th of August 1944, and published in Yiddish in "Merder fun Felker", Emes, Moscow, 1945.

FROM WARSAW TO SOBIBOR
TESTIMONY OF BER FREIBERG

When war was declared, I was living in Lodz with my family. Believing that we would be safer in a big city, we left for Warsaw. My father died on the way.

We lived in the Warsaw ghetto until January, 1941, then left for Turbin, in the vicinity of Lublin, where we remained until May, 1942. Soon we were deported and reunited with Jews in Zolkiewka. From there we were transferred to Krasnystaw and, finally, were put on a cattle train.

The journey lasted three hours and we were so overcrowded that many died of suffocation. The train stopped in the middle of a forest, and when the boxcars opened, we read: Sonderkommando Sobibor. The date: May 15, 1942.

SS men were running on the platform, shouting: *"Raus! Raus!* Women and children on one side, men on the other."* We spent the night sitting on the platform. We heard screams, the laughing of the Nazis, shots and crying from women and children. Ukrainian guards, called the "Blacks" surrounded us. I felt cold.

In the morning, the first selection took place. "Tailors, cobblers, carpenters, come forward." I obeyed.

The death factory of Sobibor looked like a big farm where everything appeared normal.

The Work

There are visions that a normal man cannot conceive of. On May 16, the small group selected in our convoy was led to a hangar full of suitcases. "Make a list of what is inside: separate underwear, dresses, children's clothes, etc.," shouted a German. I asked SS Groth where the women and children went. "You will soon be together," he answered, then added, "Sing!" As we kept silent, he threatened us. An old man said, "Let us sing," and a young woman intoned the Polish song *"Pognala Wolka."* "Again, again!" screamed Groth. Then we heard an old Jewish prayer, "Purify our hearts, oh Lord! Let us serve you better and truly." SS Wagner made a speech about the beauty of National Socialism. "If you work well, you will soon join your families; otherwise you will receive a bullet in your body." Then he added, "If one of you is ill, we have a hospital. Hey, Taraskov, you will take them there. By the way, it is a place where you will rest for ever."

I wept all night, and for weeks I wanted to believe that my family was still alive.

The Convoys

Each convoy that arrived was a nightmare. We could see the long processions of prisoners, and SS man Michel, nicknamed "the speaker," greeted them with these words, "You are leaving for the Ukraine where you will work. In order to avoid epidemics, you are going to have a disinfecting shower. Put away your clothes neatly, and remember where they are, as I shall not be with you to help to find them. All valuables must be taken to the desk."

In the summer of 1942, the number of convoys increased; many arrived from Germany, and from among the prisoners, Paul Groth chose a young girl named Ruth. She became his mistress and his servant, he said. When he was away on leave, Ruth and some other young women were executed and their clothes sent to the depot. On his return, Groth, not finding Ruth, began to drink and disturbed the well-organized order of the camp. He had to be sent away.

Of the 150 people working in the clothes depot, only fifty remained. The others were murdered or committed suicide; I tried to kill myself, but failed.

Once, Groth sent a very young man to fetch an umbrella hanging on the roof; the boy fell from a height of eight meters. He was given twenty-five lashes for his clumsiness, and was threatened to have Barry after him. Groth called his dog *Mensch* (man) and the prisoners "dogs."

The umbrella game pleased the SS so much that they repeated it several times; they wanted to see if Jews were good parachutists. Then the Nazis found new entertainment: they sewed up the lower part of the prisoners' trousers and put in rats. The victims were to stand quiet; if one of them moved, he was beaten to death. SS also shaved half of the men's heads and moustaches, and one of the eyebrows. Once a prisoner was given alcohol; when he was drunk, we carried him on a stretcher around the camp, simulating a religious funeral. Frenzel was particularly sadistic; he used to tell the young girls who were being shaved before entering the gas chambers, "Don't fear, you are so young, you will live."

Many SS kept the victims' valuables for themselves; some prisoners, like the Szpengler brothers from Pulawy, who were jewelers, were forced to make jewels for the Nazis' families.

Dutch Resistance

There was an officer among the Dutch Jews and a Ukrainian guard promised to help him organize a mass escape. But the guard betrayed the plot. Although the officer took the responsibility on himself, the SS executed the whole group in camp No. 3. In order to save bullets, the victims were decapitated.

The Longest Day

In September, 1943, a group of Soviet prisoners arrived. Polish Jews knew the camps and SS habits; the Russians knew how to use arms.

Sasha Pechersky and Leon Feldhendler prepared the escape plan. October 14 was the longest day in my life. Five minutes before the fixed hour, a young prisoner asked SS Wolf to enter the clothing depot, "We found nice clothes; and what shall we do with them?" he asked. Wolf went out to see, and was killed with an axe. SS Beckmann was stabbed in his office.

We took their weapons and attacked the arsenal. What a joy to possess arms! I ran towards the gate which was not mined. A volley of bullets greeted me and forced me to retreat. I jumped over the barbed wire, and reached the forest. Free at last! But more than half of our 600 rebels died fighting or were recaptured in the forest.

FROM TEREZIN TO SOBIBOR

TESTIMONY OF KURT THOMAS

At the end of 1941, the old fortress of Terezin, sixty-five kilometers from Prague, became a gathering center for Czechoslovakian Jews, prior to their departure to Poland.

My father, mother, sister and I came from Boskovice, in Moravia. We had hoped to stay in Terezin (or Theresienstadt) until the end of the war, because it was supposed to be a ghetto for the Jewish population. Our lodgings were damp in the winter, and very hot in summer. We lacked food and water, and disease spread, causing many deaths. We were told that a convoy would leave for Poland on April 1, 1942. My family was among them.

Piaski, the Antechamber to Sobibor

On our arrival at Piaski, near Lublin, we were sent to the ghetto, and housed in apartments without toilets. The Jewish population gave us bread and soup for the first few weeks, but their resources were soon exhausted. The houses were dreadfully crammed, and in my room there were thirteen people. I worked outdoors, and my salary consisted of a midday meal. At night I tried to smuggle potatoes into the ghetto; this was extremely dangerous and difficult, as the ghetto was strictly watched, and smugglers were killed on the spot. The German authorities were interested in the number of deaths. There were from twenty to thirty daily, due to diseases, privations and shootings. However, the ghetto population increased from 3,000 to 4,000.

Piaski, like Terezin, was a transit camp; besides famine, illness and overcrowding, we dreaded deportations.

In June, 1942, on returning from work, I found that my family was gone. A train had taken them to Sobibor and, four months later, I travelled by the same train. Boskovice to Terezin, Terezin to Piaski, Piaski to Sobibor . . . In Sobibor, I worked in camp No. 2. I still remember the SS instructions: "Tie up your shoes pair by pair, in order to find them after the shower. You will be given clean clothes. Don't be afraid. Families won't be separated, but will continue their journey eastward, and you will be working in factories."

Being a specialist in textiles, I wasn't sent to the gas chambers. My job consisted of identifying clothing material found in the luggage of the prisoners. Everything contained in the suitcases was re-used by the Reich. Special attention was given to clothes with Jewish identification which had to be removed with care. Clothing and human hair, well packed, were sent to Germany by train.

One day, bulldozers appeared and dug big ditches around camp No. 3. At first, bodies were buried; afterwards they were incinerated. Coal was used for that purpose.

Our food rations were insufficient and we were forced to steal, or we would not have lasted for more than six weeks. People too sick to work were given three days to recover; after that time, they were shot. They were gathered near the barbed wire fence and executed in cold blood.

I helped in the planning of the revolt, and I think that the number of Sobibor victims amounted to 500,000.

In the Forest

After my escape, I wandered for a month in the forest, and in November, 1943, a Polish peasant allowed me to hide in his pig sty. I remained there until July, 1944.

From time to time, the farmer brought me food, clean clothes and a shaving razor. He couldn't visit me often, as the Germans used to come to his farm. The ceiling was low, and I was unable to stand. For nine months, I remained in a crouching position, and could see the sky only from a hole in the roof.

In July, 1944, after the Liberation, I joined the partisan brigades and in 1945 I returned to Boskovice, my home town. However, I couldn't settle there, as Boskovice reminded me too much of my family and my community. I emigrated to the United States.

FROM ZOLKIEWKA TO SOBIBOR

TESTIMONY OF ITZHAK LICHTMAN

Zolkiewka is eighty kilometers from Lublin. Our community numbered 3,000 people, living in thatched wooden huts. Very few had tiled or zinc roofs. Jews lived near the market place, or were dispersed in the Polish quarter; they were mainly craftsmen and small merchants.

We didn't feel anti-Semitism; Jews and Poles enjoyed a friendly relationship. Monday was market day; peasants sold their products and bought things manufactured by the Jews. My family had a stall and sold boots, made by my father and brothers. We lived in a little wooden house, we worked hard, but we were satisfied. Life went on quietly . . .

My father wanted me to become a tailor, but I preferred to be a shoemaker. As a child, I was a pupil of Rabbi Aharon-Moshe Weinberg. I learned how to pray, to know Hebrew, Yiddish, Polish and to do arithmetic.

All the Jews in Zolkiewka knew each other and we were called by our first names, followed by a patronymic: Yankel, son of Hirsh; Breindel, daughter of Sarah, etc..

We sponsored many Zionist organizations: Gordonia, Hashomer, Poalei Zion, etc. I belonged to the last. Girls joined Beit-Yacov. Young communists, directed by Yitzhak Gutman, gathered secretly near the Peretz library

I was a member of a well-known drama circle, and our profits were donated to social welfare. We got the major Warsaw newspapers, *Haint* and *Moment,* as well as political and literary publications.

The War

Soon after the war started, Zolkiewka was occupied by the enemy. The first German troops didn't show anti-Semitism; then the Russians came, and our young communists joined the militia.

Our rabbi, Feldhendler, as the head of a delegation, asked the Soviets for permission to follow the retreating army. This was granted and we were even allowed to take our luggage. However, many Jews remained, refusing to abandon their newly built houses!

After the Russians' departure, mobs began to spread terror. Wealthy families were massacred and their property stolen; the young people who welcomed the Russians were also murdered. The mayor tried to restore order, but failed. German soldiers who entered the town laughed at the sight of dead Jews.

At first, the Nazis just stole Jewish possessions, such as furs and jewelry.[1] Then they ordered us to leave the place. Later, they rounded us up and sent us to labor camps. I was posted in Rudy, near Chelm. We lived in infested barracks, and had very little food. We had to walk sixteen kilometers to work every day. In the winter, we stopped working; the ground was frozen, and the SS kept us in the barracks. Mr. Zeidl of Zolkiewka came and "bought" us back.

But as soon as we returned to Zolkiewka, we were caught again, as were Poles. The mayor, Wac, and other Poles were sent to Majdanek. I was also arrested, but the Germans released me, saying, "Your time will come soon." It came, indeed, on May 22, 1942, when the majority of the Jewish population was deported to Sobibor.

Sobibor

We walked from Zolkiewka to Krasnystaw station. Everyone could see that we were Jews: the men wore traditional caftans and beards, women had their heads covered. Many children followed us, and Poles said as we passed, *"Hey, Zydzi, idziecie na spalenie"* (Jews, you are going to burn). We spoke Yiddish, but we also knew Polish; still, the meaning of these words escaped us. We had heard of the death camp of Belzec, but we didn't believe it.

At Krasnystaw station, Gestapo agents proceeded to a selection: they dragged out some healthy looking young men. As I wanted to stay with my family, I hid behind them. I never knew what became of the "selected" ones.

We were put into a cattle train; children looked through barred windows and reassured us, "We are not going in the direction of Belzec." We were very thirsty, and mothers became hysterical.

We had never heard of Sobibor. The Germans had succeeded in concealing the existence of that camp, better than they had for Belzec, which had been known to Jews since March.

We reached Sobibor at last. The boxcar doors opened suddenly, and the fresh air and the smell of the pine trees did us good. But what followed was horrifying; it happened so quickly that we had no time to think. We acted like automatons. *"Schnell, raus, raus, rechts, links!"* (Fast, out! Left, right!), shouted the Nazis. I held my five-year old son by the hand. A Ukrainian guard snatched him; I dreaded that the child would be killed, but my wife took him. I calmed down, believing I would see them again soon.

A kind of brute dragged me out, together with five other men. We were taken to the kitchens and handed buckets full of liquid. We were ordered to follow the guard, who suddenly told us to stop and place the buckets near the door. We heard screams; I learned later that we were at the entrance to the gas chambers.

On our way back, I met a crowd of naked women and children. I thought I recognized my wife and son, and ran towards them. The sentry hit me on the head.

We returned to the station; the men were still there. SS man Wagner was looking for craftsmen. My father pushed me forward. "I am a shoemaker." The SS asked, "Have you brought any samples?" "Yes," I replied. Truly, I had nothing to show. "Here is another shoemaker," I continued, presenting Shaul Fleishhacker, and added, "My father and brothers are also shoemakers." The SS refused. "I have enough," he said. An idea came to my head, "My wife is a dressmaker." The Nazi took her name, left, and came back. "She is already gone."

Guards took us to the barracks of the shoemakers. In a corner, we saw pieces of leather and, on a table, remains of food. Who had been here before? Soon we would stop asking that question and understand; we were in another Belzec.

An SS man gave us the measurements of the *Lagerkommandant,* and ordered a pair of shoes immediately. We obeyed and the SS man seemed pleased. *"Ihr bleibt bis zum Schluss"* (You will stay to the end). What end? The gas chambers?

We were five shoemakers: Shaul Fleishhacker from Kalisz, Shlomo, nicknamed the "Negro," Berek Lichtman, a cousin of mine, and I. In the second workshop, there were eight to ten Ukrainians, who mended the boots.

The SS ordered two pairs of boots and slippers for each of them, and shoes for their families. We wanted to live and avenge ourselves, and to see the end of Sobibor.

All workshops worked for the personal profit of the SS; they were always stealing from the State, since a Jew was only to work for the Reich or die.[1] Only one SS man showed kindness, and used to bring us bread. "One good thing is that death is awaiting us all," he said. I remember the day when a convoy arrived from Germany, and that SS officer selected more young people than were needed. Apparently, he helped a young doctor to escape; eventually, he was sent away.

Most of the Nazis were sadists. One of them wore white gloves and always made speeches. "How lucky are the ones who are leaving! They are to receive houses and properties, and are more fortunate than our own families. As soon as your work is finished here, you will receive good references and join your relatives." We thought, "Assassins, you will pay for it."

Some of these Nazis were demented. Once, an SS man ordered two groups of prisoners to cross their arms behind their backs and fight each other, like cocks.

In a Dutch convoy, the Nazis chose a hospital nurse, Mrs. Hejdi, together with her husband, her son and daughter, but they sent the husband and son to camp No. 3. The woman was sobbing. "Are you crying because your husband left you?" laughed the Nazis. They brought a Czechoslovakian middle-aged prisoner and told them, "You are husband and wife." Then they forced them to sleep together.

The Women Prisoners

Hunger, filth and black fleas ate us. One day, I summoned up enough courage to say to Wagner, "If you want us to work, we must wash our clothes." The next day, three young women were selected out of a convoy and ordered to wash our clothes. Soon their group included eighty people.

We always tried to find food. Once Wagner caught one of our carpenters eating; he flogged him and hanged him publicly in order to teach us a lesson.

The Resistance

We conceived of a strange plan: Shaul Fleishhacker, I and some others wrote on scraps of paper: "This is a death camp; let us revolt." We conveyed the message to newly arrived prisoners from Germany. The reaction was not what we expected. Some read the note and put it in a pocket; others tore it up; an elderly man shouted that it was a provocation. We had to give up our project.

The Nazis often went on vacation; we saw them filling their cases with clothes, food, and the like. We were sure it was the right time to prepare our coup.

The Convoy of Pechersky

A convoy arrived from the Soviet Union. As the Dutch prisoners had all been executed, workers were needed for camp No. 4. After a selection, eighty people remained alive, among them lieutenant Sasha Pechersky and Fiedia, nicknamed Katiush. They used to sing loudly when working, they became our friends and, together, we worked up a plan of escape and revenge.

Some prisoners showed great courage in preparing the revolt; for instance, Szmajzner managed to steal eight rifles.

84

The first Nazi to be liquidated was Falaster, in the shoe-makers' workshop. He was killed with an axe and then Shaul took his gun. We wrapped the body in a blanket and hid it.

I escaped by passing the main gate with a group of prisoners, and we reached the forest.

The Forest

Our aim was to join the partisans. A young peasant showed us the way to the Parczew forest, thirty-five kilometers from Sobi-bor. We met some Jewish fugitives and a few partisans. Life in the underground was not easy. We succeeded in buying some rifles, but we used them to frighten peasants and force them to give us food. We were always assailed by Ukrainian and Polish bandits. Because of them, not many prisoners saw the end of the war.

---

(1) There were many thefts at the time of the extermination of Jews. The SS general Fritz Katzmann, charged with the mass murder of Jews of South Galicia, complained of the soldiers' dishonesty. SS Captain Amon Goeth, in charge of the liquidation of the ghettos of Cracow and Tarnow, and commander of the camp of Plaszow, mentioned during his trial in 1946 that many Germans were stealing. The judge SS Konrad Morgen mentioned also the corruption of the SS in Auschwitz during the Frankfurt trial, 1964.

FROM HOLLAND TO SOBIBOR

TESTIMONY OF ILANA SAFRAN, ALIAS URSULA STERN-BUCHHEIM

I was born in Essen in 1926. When the Nazis came to power, my parents sold their business and took refuge in Holland.

When Holland was occupied by the Germans, we were living in Epe. My father, Albert Stern, entered the Resistance and joined a group of twenty people in the *Oranje Vrijbuiters* movement. As he knew how to handle arms, he became an instructor. His group took part in the assault on the Apeldorn town hall, and brought back food ration cards and important documents.

One of the tasks of the group consisted of hiding persecuted Jews and R. A. F. parachutists. They kept in touch with the Resistance in Utrecht, Hilversum and Rotterdam. Many Jews, provided with false identity cards, found refuge with Dutch patriots. But there were also traitors. Because of them, a policeman, Kees de Brun, was murdered by the Gestapo.

My parents' hiding place was discovered, and they were deported to Auschwitz where they died. I belonged to a group of fifteen who were hidden by the Pompe family, who could hardly afford to feed us. When our hiding place was discovered, Mrs. Pompe was sent to Ravensbruck, and only Heinz Neiman, Rudi Cohen, and Loeki Danielsen escaped the SS. I was sent to Utrecht prison with the parents and sister of Danielsen, and with Mr. Lever and his son. Then we were transferred to Amstelveen and, finally, to the camp at Vught.

From Vught to Westerbork

At Vught there were many Jewish families and many children. I was sixteen years old and made friends with some girls: Clarje de Hartog, Nanny Gokkes, Katty Gokkes of the Hague, Betty van Crefeld, Betty Heymans, Selma Wijnberg of Zwolle, Mimi Katz of Harlem. We all tried to comfort the children. Food was bad but adequate. We suffered a lot from the repetitive roll calls.

Later we were transferred to Westerbork, the gathering place of Dutch Jews, and we remained there for one week. In April, 1943, we left for Poland.

The journey to Poland was dreadful; the prisoners from western countries believed that they were going to labor camps. In 1943, the Poles already knew that Sobibor was a death camp and when they arrived there they refused to leave the train.

When we reached Sobibor, a selection took place: young girls were placed on one side, the others, including children, went to the gas chambers. We were given postcards. "Write to your families that you have arrived safely." I wrote a card to some Dutch friends; it reached its destination, and I found it after the war.

Sobibor was hell. Convoys arrived from Westerbork every Tuesday and Friday, until June, 1943. To escape! But how? For the Dutch people, it was quite impossible; we knew no Polish, no Ukrainian. Only one group of prisoners tried to escape (there were seventy-two of them), but they were recaptured and killed.

The October Revolt

The Soviet prisoners arrived in September, 1943; they established contact with the Ukrainian guards who had stopped believing in a Nazi victory and who promised to contact the partisans. Unfortunately, the plan failed.

On October 14, I knew that something was going to happen. I heard screams, and saw prisoners running towards the barbed wire. I ran too, accompanied by Katty Gokkes. We reached the forest quite easily, and met Eda Lichtman. We wandered a long time, hungry and freezing. A young man showed us the way to the partisans' camp.

Life with the Partisans

There were many types of resistance movement: Poles and Ukrainians were fighting all the time. One day, we heard Yiddish; it came from the group known as "Michal," which included Sobibor escapees.

Our life was exhausting; we walked fifty to sixty kilometers a days, but we were free . . . Once we were attacked by Poles who took our arms. "You have taken the weapons that the Allies have parachuted to us," they said.

Our main activity consisted of sabotaging trains. We also sheltered women and children and fed them. At last, we met Russian partisans — a real army of 2,000; but they refused to accept us all. They were only interested in the young ones, and promised to give the girls military training. As we wanted to be together, it was very hard. We fought against the Germans and, just before the Liberation, Katty Gokkes lost her life.

After the Liberation, we travelled to Wlodawa, and I met Selma Wijnberg and her fiancé, Haim Engel. We returned to Sobibor, but all traces of the camp had disappeared. The next stops were Lublin, Chernovitz, Odessa and, finally, Holland. I wanted to escape Europe. Now I live and work in Ashdod, in Israel!

THE REVOLT AT SOBIBOR
TESTIMONY OF ALEXANDER PECHERSKY

In the autumn of 1943, the Germans started to evacuate the Jewish population of Minsk. The last inhabitants of the ghetto were at first transferred to labor camps in Sheroka Street where they joined 500 Jewish craftsmen, 100 war prisoners, Soviet Jews and 300 non-Jews who were punished for not respecting German orders.

We used to get up at 5 A.M. and finished work at 6 P.M. Everyday we got two rations of bread of 150 grams each, and some soup. The commander was always inventing new games to humiliate us.

Transfer to Sobibor

In September, 1943, we were told that Jews would be transferred to Germany, but that families would not be separated. At 4 A.M. a silent crowd left Minsk, the men on foot, women and children in trucks. We gathered at the railway station where a freight train awaited us. Seventy people were crowded into a boxcar, and after four days we reached Sobibor. We stopped during the night and were given water. The doors opened, and facing us, was a poster: Sonderkommando Sobibor.

Tired and hungry, we left the car. Armed SS officers stood there and *Oberscharführer* Gomerski shouted: "Cabinet makers and carpenters with no families, forward." Eighty men were led into the camp and locked in a barrack.

Older prisoners informed us about Sobibor. We had all fought in the war and had suffered in labor camps, but we were so horrified about Sobibor that we could not sleep that night. Shlomo Leitman, a Polish Jew from Sheroka, was lying at my side. "What will become of us?" he asked. I didn't answer, pretending to sleep. I couldn't get over my reaction and was thinking of Nelly, a little girl who travelled in my boxcar and who was, no doubt, dead already. I thought of my own daughter Elochka.

On September 24, I wrote in my diary: "We are in the camp of Sobibor; we rise at 5:00 A.M., get a liter of warm water, but no bread; at 5:30, we are counted; at 6:00 we leave for work, in columns of threes. Russian Jews are in front, then Poles, Czech and Dutch."

I remember when the SS man Frenzel ordered us to sing; Cybulski was walking at my side. "What shall we sing?" he asked and I answered, "We know only one song: *Yesli Zavtra Voyna.*" It was a patriotic Russian song and it gave us hope for freedom.

Soldiers led us to the Nordlager, a new section of the camp. Nine barracks were already built there and others were under construction. Our group was split in two: one part was sent to build, the other to cut wood. On our first day of work, fifteen people got twenty-five lashes each for incompetence.

On September 25, we unloaded coal all day, and were given only twenty minutes for lunch. The cook was unable to feed us all in such a short time. Frenzel was furious and ordered the cook to sit down. Then he whipped him while whistling a march tune. The soup tasted as though it had been mixed with blood and, although we were very hungry, many of us were unable to eat.

The Inmates of Sheroka

I was born in Kremenchug in 1919, but spent my childhood in Rostov. After I finished my secondary studies, I entered a music school. Music and theater were the most important things in my life. I directed amateur dramatic circles and took a great interest in the arts.

In 1941, I joined the army with the rank of second lieutenant, and was soon promoted to first lieutenant. Taken prisoner in October 1941, I caught typhus, but concealed the disease, fearing to be killed.

In May, 1942, I tried to escape with four other prisoners, but we were caught and were sent, first to the disciplinary camp of Borysov, and then to Minsk. During a medical examination, it was discovered that I was Jewish. I was locked up with other Jews in a place nicknamed "the Jewish cellar," where we spent ten days in complete darkness. We were allowed 100 grams of bread a day and a jug of water. Then, on September 20, 1942, we were transferred to the labor camp of Sheroka Street, in Minsk, where I lived until my deportation to Sobibor.

Our arrival at the camp made a great impression on the older prisoners; they knew well that the war was going on, but had never seen the men who fought in it. And these newcomers could handle arms! We were approached by men and women who made us understand that their wish was to get out of hell.

I couldn't speak Yiddish so Shlomo Leitman, who was born in Warsaw, acted as interpreter. We could understand some Polish as it resembles Russian.

I wanted to know the topography of Sobibor. Camp No. 1, where we lived, included workshops and kitchens; camp No. 2, the reception center of the new arrivals, had storage for the belongings stolen from the prisoners; a corridor led to camp No. 3 and its gas chambers.

On September 26, twenty-five prisoners were whipped; a young Dutchman, tall and lean, was chopping wood, but was not strong enough for the task. The SS guard hit him on the head. Astonished I stopped working. Furious, the guard shouted, "I give you five minutes to chop this wood; if you fail, you will get twenty-five lashes." I hit the wood as though it were his head. "You did it in four and a half minutes," said the Nazi, looking at his watch. He offered me a cigarette. "Thanks, I don't smoke," I replied.

27 September. We were still working at the Nordlager. At 9 A.M. Kali-Mali, from Sheroka, whose real name was Shubayev, told me, "All the Germans have left, only the Kapo is here; why?" I answered, "I don't know, but let us see where we are." A prisoner informed us, "If they are not here, it means that a convoy has just arrived; look over there, at the camp No. 3." We heard a terrible scream from a woman, followed by children wailing, "Mother, mother!" And, as if to add to the horror, the bawling of geese joined the human wailing. A farmyard was established in

the camp to enrich the menus of the SS men, and the bawling of the geese covered the shrieks of the victims.

My helplessness at these crimes horrified me; Shlomo Leitman and Boris Cybulski were livid. "Sasha, let us escape, we are only 200 meters from the forest; we can cut the barbed wire with our axes and run." said Boris. "We must escape all together and soon; winter is near and snow is not our friend," he added.

On September 28, one week after I arrived at the camp, I knew everything about the hell of Sobibor. Camp No. 4 was on a hill; each section was surrounded with barbed wire and was mined. I was informed of the exact place occupied by the personnel, the guards and the arsenal.

Next day, the 600 prisoners, men and women, were taken to the station to unload eight cars of bricks. Each of us was forced to run and fetch eight bricks; the one who failed was whipped twenty-five times. We finished our work in less than an hour and we returned to our commandos. The reason for the haste: a new convoy was just entering the station.

Our group of eighty men was finally led to camp No. 4. I was working near Shlomo; another prisoner from Sheroka approached me and whispered, "We have decided to escape; there are only five SS officers, and we can wipe them out. The forest is near." I replied, "Easier said than done; the five guards are not together. When you finish with one, the second shoots at us; and how shall we cross the minefields? Wait, the time is near."

At night, Baruch told me, "It is not the first time that we have planned to finish with Sobibor, but very few of us know how to use arms. Lead us, and we shall follow you." His intelligent face inspired trust and gave me courage. I asked him to form a group of the most reliable prisoners.

On October 7, I gave to Baruch my first instructions on how to dig a tunnel: "The carpenters' workshop is at the end of the camp, five meters from the barbed wire; the net of three rows of barbed wire occupies four meters to fifteen meters; let us add seven meters, the length of the barrack. We shall start digging under the stove and the tunnel will be no more than thirty-five meters long and eighty centimeters deep, because of the danger of mines. We shall have at least twenty cubic meters of earth to hide, and shall leave that earth under the floorboards. The job must be done only at night."

We all agreed to start working; the digging of the tunnel would take us fifteen to twenty days. But the plan presented weak spots: between 11 P.M. and 5 A.M. six hundred persons had to pass in Indian file the thirty-five meters of the tunnel and run a good distance from the camp in order to avoid the posse of the SS. I said, "I also have other ideas; meanwhile, let us prepare our first arms: seventy well whetted knives or razor blades." Baruch said that the kapos were interested in our plans and could be very helpful, since they walked freely in the camp. I thought that their help was vital. "All right, I accept," I said.

October 8, 1943. A new transport arrived. Janek, the carpenters' supervisor, needed three prisoners to help him: Shlomo, another prisoner and I were chosen and sent to camp No. 1. That same evening, Baruch brought Shlomo seventy well whetted knives.

October 9: Grisha, who was caught sitting while cleaning wood, got twenty-five lashes. It was a bad day: thirty of our people had been flogged for various transgressions and we were exhausted. In the evening, Kali-Mali came to the barracks, out of breath. He informed me that Grisha and seven of our men were ready to escape and asked us to join them. "Come with us; the site near the barbed wire is badly lit; we will kill the guard with an axe and then we will run to the forest." We went to find Grisha, and I explained to him that reprisals would be terrible even if his plan succeeded; I had to use threats before I persuaded him to plan only a collective escape.

October 10: I saw an SS officer with his arm in a sling. I was told that it was Greishutz, back from his leave. He had been wounded in a Russian air raid. Later, Shlomo and I met the kapo Brzecki who knew that we were preparing something. "Take me with you; together we shall accomplish more. I know the end awaits us all," he said, and he also asked us to include the kapo Geniek. I answered, "Could you kill a Nazi?" He thought for a moment, and replied, "Yes, if it is necessary for our cause."

October 11: That morning, we heard screams followed by shots. We were locked up in the barracks and guards stood around us. The shooting lasted a long time and seemed to be coming from the Nordlager. We feared that the prisoners had tried to escape before we were ready. Soon we learned the cause of the fusillade: a group of new prisoners already undressed, had revolted and had tried to run in the direction of the barbed wire. The guards began to shoot and killed many of them instantly. The others were dragged to camp No. 3. That day, the crematorium burned longer than usual. Huge flames rose up in the grey autumn sky and the camp was lit with strange colors. Helpless and distressed, we looked at the bodies of our brothers and sisters.

October 12: It was a terrible day; eighteen of our friends, many from Sheroka, were sick. Several SS men, under the direction of Frenzel, entered our barrack and asked the patients to follow them. Among them was a young Dutch prisoner with his wife, and the unfortunate man could hardly walk. The woman was running after the group screaming, "Murderers, I know where you are taking my husband; I can't live without him! Assassins, murderers!" She died with the group.

Shlomo and I ordered a meeting for 9:00 P.M. at the carpenters' workshop. Baruch, Shlomo, Janek, the tailors Joseph and Jacob, Moniek and others were present. We posted a sentry at the entrance. Moniek went out to fetch Brzecki and, when both returned, I asked Brzecki again if he had thought over the consequences of his decision; if the plan failed, he would be the first to die. He said, "I know it, but we must get rid of the SS officers and this should take one hour. If we could do it in less time, so much the better. For that purpose, we need efficient and determined men, since one moment's hesitation would be fatal, and I know some capable people who can do the job." At 3:00 P.M., Brzecki was to lead three of his men to camp No. 2 under any pretext that he would find himself. Their task would consist of liquidating the four officers present. Baruch would lead the SS men to a place where the prisoners would be waiting, and would prevent anyone from leaving camp No. 2 once the action had begun.

At exactly 4 o'clock, another team would cut the telephone wires from camp No. 2 to the guards' quarters. The same team would hide those wires in such a way as to make it impossible to reconnect the telephone on the same day.

At the same time, we were to start killing SS officers; they would be invited, one by one, into the workshops where two of our men would execute them. At 4:30 P.M., everything would be finished. At the same time, Brzecki and Geniek would assemble the prisoners for the usual evening roll call. In front would be the

Soviet prisoners who were to take over the arsenal and the rest of us would cover them. Once the arsenal was open, armed men would head the group and kill the guards at the gate. If they resisted, we would fight with the arms taken from the officers.

Near the workshops and the officers' villas was a mesh of barbed wire. There the ground was mined, but less dangerous. Stones were to be thrown in order to destroy the mines.

Those were the details of the plan; I added that I had long discussions with Shlomo and I couldn't think of anything better. I asked everybody to think it over again, and a new meeting was planned for the next day, under the strictest secrecy.

Just before the revolt, an idea occurred to me and I wanted to check if it was right. Having observed the behavior of the guards for a long time, I knew that every morning each of them got five bullets for his rifle. I also noticed that, with the changing of each guard, the bullets were handed over to the next guard. This meant that the guards who were not on duty had no bullets. In order to check my findings, I asked Brzecki to find an excuse to send me to the guards' barracks. On October 13, at 10:00 A.M., the carpentry workshop got an order to send a man to the barracks in order to repair the doors. Janek sent me there and, while I was visiting the rooms, I was glad to see that my idea was correct.

October 14: "On the night of October 13, we distributed knives and hatchets, as well as warm clothes." I was to remain in the carpentry workshop where, from the window, I could watch what was happening in camp No. 3. In the next barrack, Shlomo and a team of twenty men were repairing our wooden beds.

According to our plan, at 4:00 and at 4:15 P.M., two SS men were to appear at the tailors' workshop. At the same time, two officers, Greischutz and Goetzinger were in another workshop. Frenzel was supervising the building of some cupboards. Rosenfeld's job was to kill him. Friedrich Gaulatisch would enter the carpentry workshop where Shlomo would be waiting. Other SS officers of camp No. 2 were to be enticed into different workshops.

Each of us had his task: Shubayev, aged twenty-five, a railway engineer from Rostov, a good and simple buddy, would go to the tailors' workshop with Moniek, Cybulski, a thirty-five year old driver, a former truck driver from Donbass, and accompanied by Michael and Benyo. Guided by Brzecki, they were to go to camp No. 2, to meet Baruch.

At 2 P.M., SS *Untersharführer* Walter Ryba came to Brzecki; he had a machine gun, and that worried me. That morning, Grenzel noticed that Janek was better dressed than usual, but Geniek reassured us. Brzecki had to go to camp No. 4 with other prisoners in order to stack wood. The guard took his machine gun only because he was the sole supervisor.

Geniek was to lead the four men to camp No. 2. At first, he asked us to postpone it to the next day, but that was impossible. Although the details of our plan were known only to the committee and a small group, the other prisoners felt that something was going to happen, and kept asking: "Well, when will it be?"

On the eve of October 14th, the older people said prayers: It was Yom Kippur, the day of Atonement. Some inmates told them, "Better pray for Sasha to help you." They answered, "We are praying to God to help Sasha."[1]

We had another reason for not postponing our plan: On October 14, Gomerski was on vacation. The *Lagerführer* Frenzel was a bastard but, compared to Gomerski, he seemed a choir boy. "Tomorrow may be too late," I said to Geniek, "we have to do what we decided, and you must obey."

At 3:20 P.M., Geniek came to Cybulski's barrack with Shlomo and the two others. Two officers were killed by Weisspapier in the shoemakers' barrack while Jacob was giving them their boots. At 4:15, I heard that Cybulski, Michael and Baruch had accomplished their mission at camp No. 2. At 4 P.M., I had met Luka, the Dutch girl and told her, "The officers will soon be dead; be ready to escape." As she trembled, I added, "What we are doing is the only way to survive; we have no right to give up living, we must avenge ourselves."

At 4:30 P.M., Brzecki returned from camp No. 4, with the commando, and *Unterscharführer* Gaulatisch arrived soon afterwards. Shlomo told him, "We have done the repairs in the barracks; now the workers don't know what to do." The SS man went in; Shlomo's hatchet awaited him.

Frenzel didn't come, and later we learned that SS officer Ryba had been killed in the garage.

Now it was vital to leave; Brzecki whistled and prisoners were directed to camp No. 1 in a disorderly way. This infuriated the

The railroad station in the village.

Watchtower, former observation post for forest fires.

From the railroad station to the camp.

Tomasz Blatt *Simha Bialowitz* *Hella Felenbaum-Weiss*

Stanislaw Szmajzner *Moshe Bahir*

Eda and Itzhak Lichtman

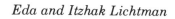

Abraham Margulies (left)

Hella Weiss (right)
with Soviet partisans

Itzhak Lichtman and Ber Freiberg

Joseph Dunietz

Kurt Thomas

Aizik Rottenberg

M. Goldfarb

Yehuda Lerner

Alexander Pechersky

Joseph Zukerman

Haim Lejst

Samuel Lerer

Simon Rosenthal and Sasha Pechersky (right)

Meir Ziss

Zelda Metz-Kelberman

Shlomo Podchlebnik

Leon Feldhendler (stand
ing, right). Seated, from
right to left: *Yehuda
Lerner, Esther Rab, Shlo
mo and Zelda Metz
Kelberman*

Haïm Treger
(right)
with his family

Ilana Safran   *Jacob Biskubicz*

Two of the guards

Odilo Globocnik (center)

Gotlieb Hering (right) *and Heinrich Glei, of the Operation Reinhard.*

Gustav Felereng and H. Glei

Erwin Lambert (constructor of the gas chambers)

Members of Einsatz Reinhard

Anton Nowak

Hermann Michel

Paul Groth

Richard Thomalla

W. Blaurick

Franz Wolf

guard, a *Volksdeutsch* from the Volga region; he was killed with an axe.

A new group, coming from camp No. 2, entered camp No. 1 where prisoners were just learning what was happening. A Ukrainian guard began to shoot; a mighty "Hurrah" was heard. "Forward! forward!" shouted the prisoners. They were running towards the gate, shooting with rifles, cutting barbed wire with pliers. We crossed a minefield and many lost their lives. My group marched towards the quarter where the SS lived, and several of us were killed. Between the camp and the forest there was an immense clearing and here, too, many fell.

At last, we got to the forest, but Shlomo and Luka were missing. We walked all night in a column, one by one; I was up front, followed by Cybulski, while Arkady brought up the rear. We were all silent; from time to time, a light was visible in the sky. After walking three kilometers we reached a canal, that was five or six meters wide and quite deep. Suddenly we saw a group of men; Arkady went crawling off to investigate. He found Shubayev and many other friends. Together we built a bridge with tree trunks, and then I learned that Shlomo had been wounded while escaping. Unable to run, he asked to be put to death. Of course, nobody listened to him, and he stayed behind with other prisoners.

Our group numbered fifty-seven people. After walking another five kilometers, we heard the noise of a train. We were on the edge of a wood, an area of bushes in front of us. Dawn was approaching, and we needed a safe place to hide. I knew that the Nazis were after us and we thought that a group of trees near a railway wouldn't attract the attention of our enemy. We decided to remain there during the day, camouflaged by branches.

At dawn, it was raining. Arkady and Cybulski left to explore the terrain on one side, Shubayev and I on the other. We found an abandoned site near the forest. Cybulski and Arkady reached the railway line. Poles were working there, but without a guard.

We hid and posted two sentries nearby; these sentries were to be changed every three hours. All day, planes were flying over our heads. We heard the voices of the Polish workers. At night, we saw two men looking for something; we understood that they were fugitives who had returned from the direction of Bug. "Why haven't you crossed the river?" I asked. They told us that they had been near a village where they learned that soldiers were sent along the Bug River to check all points. I asked if they had met Luka, and they assured me that they had seen her in the forest, leaving for Chelm with Polish Jews. We formed a new column, Cybulski and I leading, Arkady and Shubayev in the rear. After five kilometers we reached the forest, but we couldn't find enough food so we decided to split into small groups, each taking a different direction. My unit included Shubayev, Cybulski, Arkady, Michael Itzkovich and Simon Mazurkewich.

We set off eastwards, guided by the stars. We walked at night, and hid during the day. Our objective was to cross the Bug river. We approached little villages to beg for food and to ask our way. We were often told, "Prisoners escaped from Sobibor where people are being burned; they are looking for fugitives."

We reached the village of Stawki, a kilometer and a half from the Bug river. We had spent the day in the forest and, at sunset, three of us entered a hut. A thirty-year old peasant was cutting and gathering tobacco leaves; an old man was near a stove. In a corner, a baby's cradle was hanging from the ceiling, and a young woman was rocking it.

"Good evening, may we come in?" "Come in, come in," answered the young man. "Draw the curtains," said Cybulski. We sat down; everyone was quiet. "Could you tell us where to cross the Bug?" asked Shubayev. "I don't know," said the young man. "You must know; you have been living here long enough. We know that there are places where the water is low, and the crossing easy," I said. "If you are so sure, then go. We know nothing, and we have no right to go near rivers."

We talked a little longer, and told them that we were escaped war prisoners and wished to return home. At last, the young man said, "I shall show you the direction, but I won't go to the river. Find it yourselves. Be careful; it is guarded everywhere since prisoners escaped from a camp where soap is made with human fat. The fugitives are being chased everywhere, even underground. If you are lucky, you will get to the other side. I wish you luck."

"Let's go before the moon rises." "Wait" said the young woman, "take some bread for the way." We thanked them and the old man blessed us with the sign of the cross.

The same night, October 19, we crossed the Bug. On the 22nd, eight days after the uprising, we met a unit of partisans of the Voroshilov detachment. A new chapter began.

[1]Pechersky was mistaken: It was not Yom Kippur, it was Sukkoth. (Ed. note).

FROM ZAMOSC TO SOBIBOR
TESTIMONY OF LEA REISNER-BIALOWITZ

I was born in Zamosc, to a well-to-do business family. At the age of twelve I already looked like a grown-up woman, and that probably saved my life. The first time Jews were rounded up, I was sent to Janowice, a labor camp, with 80 other women and 200 men. Our supervisors were two SS officers, Jan Pinkowski and Ludwig. In the camp, my cousin, Aron Reizman, was killed by Pinkowski.

Our camp was a one-hour's walk from Zamosc. We got soup and bread for our work. My father was in the Siebs factory and my mother cleaned the barracks. In Zamosc itself, two SS officers, Rollmann and Kolb spread terror. My uncle, Wolf Reisner, was murdered by Rollmann.

The ghetto was situated in the Nowe-Miasto quarter and conditions were horrifying. After the death of my uncle, my aunt and her three daughters came to us, and they lived in the same room with us — my parents, my brothers and I.

While we were in the labor camp, Rollmann, Kolb, Riebenschein and a Captain Fritz were to chase old people and children and deport them. Nobody knew where they went.

Easter 1942: Pinkowski sent us to Janowice. When we returned, we learned that hundreds of our people had been deported to an unknown destination. In the autumn, a decree ordered our transfer from Zamosc to Izbica. We walked all the way and the weak were killed systematically. The Jews from Zolkiewka, Turbin, Krasnystaw and Piaski were assembled in Izbica. Thousands of Jews from other countries joined us. The

Izbica ghetto was a veritable anthill in which the Nazis enjoyed harassing us. SS man Engel killed people while they slept in their beds or were just walking in the streets. He killed small children as well.

Life was a nightmare, and the fear of being arrested was worse than death. We were always hungry, and my mother exchanged her last possessions for bread. When we heard the cry of alarm "Die Deutschen" (the Germans), we left the streets of the ghetto and hid in the cellars. Exhausted, my mother insisted that my brother and I must run away. "Go to a village; there must be some kind people somewhere; your life may be saved," she said. The moment we got to the other side of the ghetto, an SS officer saw us. He shot and killed my brother. I reached the forest all alone and found some fugitives. We spent the days lying on the ground, and at night we stole potatoes in the fields.

Return to Izbica

The peasants we met were kind, but were too frightened to help us. They said, "There is a new ghetto in Izbica; you can't spend the winter here, you will die." Desperate, I returned to Izbica, but my parents were gone. I was sheltered by the Bialowitz family. We lived miserably, without food, without clothes, and worked in a factory. In the spring, we were deported to Sobibor.

Sobibor

I shall never forget the inscription in big black letters when we arrived at the camp. Ten people were selected, including the two Bialowitz brothers and me. Frenzel and Wolf carried out the selection. Hungry and feverish, I was sent to the laundry; I knew that death was awaiting if I stopped. Once Frenzel kicked me with his boots because I dared to put on a headscarf to protect myself against the cold.

When convoys came to Sobibor, I trembled with horror at seeing young women, with children in their arms, walking innocently to their death.

101

One day, Simha told me that something was being prepared and that soon we would be free. The plan of the revolt was very simple: to kill the SS one at a time.

When we reached the arms depot, the Ukrainian guard had begun to shoot from the watchtower; then the brute, Frenzel, took his machine gun and shot at us, non-stop.

I reached the forest and hid; all night, the enraged SS chased us; I wondered how I could survive the winter in the forest. I lived on raw potatoes, and managed to spend some nights in a stable.

At last, I reached Radeczny; there was a monastery which I knew by name, because our old servant used to visit it. I learned that the Germans had left the country, and I travelled to Zamosc where I found my old house occupied by Poles from Poznan. I met my old servant, and she screamed on seeing me again; she took me for a ghost!

Later I found Simha, who had managed to escape; we married and left for Israel.

FROM WLODAWA TO SOBIBOR

TESTIMONY OF AIZIK ROTTENBERG

I was born in the little town of Wlodawa; we were ten children in our family. Wlodawa had 8,000 Jews, but, today, no more than perhaps 50 remain alive. Wlodawa, although far away from Warsaw, had a very active political and cultural life. All parties were represented; clubs and associations enabled us to practice all kinds of sport, and we also contributed to the theater. We had a Yeshiva, one of the oldest and most famous in Poland. It was in our town that the well-known rabbi of Radzin found refuge and called for resistance. The poet, Katzenelson, wrote a poem about him.

Wlodawa was about eight kilometers from Sobibor. Polish peasants who went to market were saying, "Jews, young and old, are being burned in Sobibor." Nobody believed that such a thing could happen in the 20th century, but the peasants brought us more and more proof.

You may ask, "What were you waiting for, being only eight kilometers from the crematorium?" Where could we go? We were trapped and terrified of the SS who occupied Wlodawa, and were shooting at random in the streets.

There were also the Gestapo people, the S.D., the *Schupos,* those who wore armbands and swastikas; there were also the "navy blue", the Polish police who collaborated with the Germans; let alone the "Blacks," Ukrainian volunteers, and all the other anti-Semites. We expected pogroms, and we were aware of the greed of those who were impatient to rob us of our meager savings.

You may also wonder why 8,000 people did not fight the Nazis. But a hundred men armed with machine guns are more powerful than an unarmed crowd. The young ones would have tried to escape, but refused to abandon their parents; they knew it would mean the death of the older people, and how was it possible to leave behind the helpless little brothers and sisters without support?

The Way to Sobibor

In November 1942, the first deportation from Wlodawa to Sobibor took place. I went there on May 1, 1943. My father was already dead. A glazier by trade, he had travelled much and had seen many people. He was denounced to the Gestapo by an "Aryan" customer for criticising the occupation forces; the Lublin Gestapo shot him.

In the ghetto, we hoped that the war would end soon, and we built underground bunkers. During the German roundup of November, 1942, the SS didn't find us: there were at least 150 of us in the bunker. But they came back to Wlodawa and found our hiding place, killing many of us.

When we arrived at Sobibor, Frenzel selected eighteen young men. Why did he choose me and one of my brothers, while the rest went to their death? I don't know, and that question still haunts me. My brother fell during the revolt; I survived. I was sent to work as a bricklayer. The Nazis wanted to live in comfort and made us build a mess, a bakery, and two ovens; I also worked on the construction of an arsenal. Starting with the end of summer, arms were delivered to Sobibor; they were first deposited in camp No. 4 and cleaned, then sent to the arsenal.

We were permanently terrorized. Once, a prisoner was talking to a Ukrainian guard; an SS man killed him. Another time we carried sand to decorate the garden; Frenzel took out his revolver, and shot a prisoner working at my side. Why? I still don't know.

One day, a convoy arrived, and half of the passengers were already dead. As I worked on the platform, I said to a woman who looked feverish, "You will soon feel better." Frenzel heard me. He hit me in the face with his whip and shot the woman dead.

I saw many convoys from Western Europe and Holland; the prisoners looked calm, thinking that they would feel better in the camp. The SS greeted them with smiles, helping the women with children, and gathering families together.

The Revolt

Like all prisoners, I dreamt of freedom, and knew well, as a Yiddish proverb says, that I was "between fire and water." Escape from Sobibor — but where? I remembered that when we arrived at the camp we had walked in rows, following a guard armed with a machine gun. Behind was a second machine gun and, all the way, guards with rifles.

On October 14, the revolt took place. I ran to the forest with my companions, and met a naked fugitive. "Come with me," I said, and gave him my coat. We looked for partisans, but didn't find any; then we were arrested by *Schupos* who didn't wish to kill us right away. They took us to Adampole, and a German called Zelinger, tied us up with chains in a stable; for weeks, he treated us like dogs. However, we managed to break the chains and escaped to the forest of Parczew. We met a group of Polish partisans who didn't want to accept us. Later we found Jewish partisans, the Yehiel group who were part of Chyl Grynspan's unit. They accepted us, and we took part in several battles.

Finally, I left for Israel where I raised a family. I am still a bricklayer.

FROM KUROW TO SOBIBOR

TESTIMONY OF HERSHEL ZUKERMAN

As soon as the war began, Kurow was bombed and the Jewish district was almost destroyed. Those who took refuge in the Blonie district were also bombed. A few days earlier, our rabbi had asked us to hide the Holy Scrolls in a cave. That's how the Torahs were saved.

We improvised temporary shelters but, shortly afterwards, the *Volksdeutschs* and the German army started looting. The Nazis organized forced labor. I managed to place my family in the village of Borowisk and, with Salomon Nussenbaum, bought a horse and a cart. Disguised as Poles, we travelled from village to village, selling and buying food, and in that way we could feed our families.

We risked our life everyday: a Jew wasn't allowed to own a horse and travel without a permit. During Easter, 1942, on my way to Kurow, I saw SS officers surrounding the district so I warned my brother and the other people whom I met, and quickly returned to Borowisk. Next day, a peasant told me that the Jewish population had been sent to Konska Wola where, for three days, they were left without food and water. Then they were deported to Sobibor. I learned that Avigdor Jacob, having refused to board the train, was killed on the platform. The daughter of Mendel Rosenbaum sent a young Pole to follow the convoy, and he reported that the train left for a forest, in the region of Chelm, not far from the river Bug.

After the first large deportation, there were officially thirty Jews left in Kurow. Some families were hiding, but not for long. They were deported after Easter, 1942, and among them my own family. We stopped at Opole where we were sent to a synagogue.

Only Haim Pesah, his wife and children managed to escape. Opole was a transit center before the deportations to Sobibor. One day, the SS officers of Pulawy, using the excuse of inadequate hygiene, sent the women and children to barracks out of town. Two of my own children were snatched. Shortly afterwards, Polish Jews were replaced by Jews from Czechoslovakia. At that time, I lost my wife and another child and, with my last son Joseph, we decided to join our family.

We walked to the station in a column; on our way, between Opole and Wanwilice, peasants stood with shovels. When they saw a well-dressed man in the crowd, they pointed him out to the Germans or Ukrainian guards and handed them a bottle of vodka. The unfortunate prisoner was killed and the peasant who "bought" the Jew took his clothes, boots, and all his belongings.

At Nalenczow, a train was waiting: 120 people were put into a car and we left for Sobibor. On our arrival, 100 men were selected, among them my son Joseph. The others went to camp No. 3. The next day, the SS asked, "Who can cook?" My son and I volunteered; we remained alive while the other 98 went to the gas chambers.

The gas chambers were so well camouflaged that for ten weeks I believed that my fellow prisoners who came with me were in a labor camp. In our kitchen we cooked the soup for camp No. 3 and Ukrainian guards used to fetch the vessels. Once I put a note in Yiddish into a dumpling, "Brother, let me know what you are doing." The answer arrived, stuck to the bottom of the pot, "You shouldn't have asked. People are being gassed, and we must bury them." I informed my two friends, Leon Feldhendler and Shlomo Goldstein. However, we decided to keep quiet, as we didn't want the others to know. One day, the Ukrainian Koszewadski, from Kiev, who supervised the kitchens, whispered to me, "I have friends among the Russian partisans and a plan to free us all." I didn't reply, but I consulted Feldhendler and Shlomo. We decided not to answer. Later on, Koszewadski confided, "I am going to Chelm to see my friend. If the Germans ask for me, tell them that I am in the camp." On his return, we told him that nobody had asked for him. He said, "My friend belongs to a partisan unit called 'Wanda Wasilewska', and there is a doctor in Chelm working with the Resistance." He wasn't lying.

The Poisoning

Thirteen people worked in the prisoners' kitchen, two in the SS officers' kitchen, and two in the Ukrainians' kitchen. We wanted to find a poison that would take effect after three or four hours. That was the time needed to meet the partisans approaching our camp, and together we would destroy Sobibor. But an order arrived from Majdanek, preventing prisoners from working in the SS kitchens. We gave some money to Koszewadski for the partisans and, one day, he ran away.

Himmler's Visit

In the winter of 1943, we learned of the impending visit of Himmler to Sobibor. On the eve of the visit, while I went out to fetch coal for the kitchen, I saw lorries with women and heard a voice calling my name. I lifted my head and saw the daughter of a friend. She was among the 300 women brought specially to entertain Himmler and his retinue with the spectacle of their death.

We were always thinking of a revolt, but wanted it to be well organized. Some previous attempts had been followed by terrible reprisals. For example, after the escape of twenty prisoners, twenty others were shot. Another time, while out in the village with a guard, two inmates offered him vodka, killed him and ran away. Twenty-seven prisoners were murdered in reprisal. A group of seventy Dutch prisoners had prepared a collective escape with a Ukrainian guard who had promised to help. But he betrayed them, and all were shot. On another day, we were told not to cook any more for the 300 prisoners of camp 3; they had been executed after attempting to revolt. Afterwards, 300 doctors, engineers, and members of liberal professions replaced the ones who were killed. These new prisoners dug a tunnel under the barbed wire, but were discovered by the SS.

One day, prisoners from a convoy were shot on the platform instead of being gassed, and a note in Yiddish was found in the pocket of a victim, "Brothers, don't believe the lies of the SS. We have come from Belzec where thousands of Jews were murdered, and on their graves a forest was planted." All those attempts taught us that an escape needed very good planning and the utmost secrecy.

A new convoy of Soviet P.O.W. arrived from Minsk and one man Sasha, made an excellent impression on us. He was to become head of the committee organizing the revolt. We met in the kitchen and our first idea was to take over the arsenal. But, as that was not practical, we decided on a silent liquidation of the SS while the guards were away. We fixed the date of October 14, when Wagner and Gomerski would be away, and we chose a password: "Now or never." Our committee consisted of ten men, and each had to keep six prisoners posted, so that sixty of us would know the time and details of the revolt. The others would be kept in the dark until the fixed day.

Between 4:00 and 4:45 P.M., seventeen SS and Ukrainian guards were killed. We were drunk with joy, and felt new strength. We shouted to each other, "Jews, this is not a roll call, it's a revolt; let us escape." My group ran towards the gate, because we knew that the ground wasn't mined and there was no ditch to be traversed. A prisoner threw salt in the eyes of a Nazi, killed him with a hatchet, and took away his revolver. At first, the Ukrainians did not shoot but it didn't last long. They started shooting on the mines. However, 300 reached the forest. My son Joseph and I ran all night.

Only thirty-five of us survived to see the end of the war. The others were killed by Germans in the forest, by Polish anti-Semites, or by robbers who took our trousers and shoes. My son and I hid for three months in the forests and swamps. From time to time, we had the courage to approach a peasant and ask for food. In November, we discovered a hiding place, a ditch that was well camouflaged in the forest. There we found Haim Pesah, his wife and two children, Manes Rochelman, the daughter and son of Aizik Schneider and a little boy. They all came from our town, and we cried with joy. We left them and looked for another hiding place; we found it, not far from Kurow, in Wijak's household. In December, we returned to the ditch to learn that Haim Pesah and his friends had been massacred by local anti-Semites.

A peasant offered to help us, but those who had killed Haim Pesah and his friends learned of our presence, and dragged us from our hiding place. They were afraid to kill us immediately, as shots would attract German soldiers. We managed to escape, and we hid again.

My son met a partisan unit and fought in the region of Lewartow. Disguised as a Polish peasant, I wandered in the forests. After the Liberation, I found my son in Lublin, and didn't want to return to Kurow. After many more journeys, we settled in the United States, where my son died.

To survive Sobibor does not mean living.

THE UPRISING OF SOBIBOR
TESTIMONY OF YEHUDA LERNER

I was born in Warsaw in a family of six; my father was a baker. When war was declared, our life in the ghetto was similar to that of most Jews: unemployment, hunger and anguish. On July 22, 1943, tragedy began in the ghetto. The president of the Jewish council committed suicide and, on the same day, my father, my mother, one of my brothers and I were taken away to the *Umschlagplatz,* the ghetto station, and were left in a building. My whole family was deported and never came back.

I was sent to a camp near Smolensk, in occupied Russia, where I remained for ten months. Our job consisted of building an airfield. For our work, we got a piece of bread and a bowl of soup. Hunger weakened us and prisoners who had no strength to work were taken to a wood and executed. Haim, a friend from the Warsaw ghetto, was with me. There also were German Jews, in transit through Warsaw. I told my friend, "Let us escape, we are doomed here."

Four months later, on a dark night, we crossed the barbed wire, but we were caught and sent to another camp where we again found hard work, hunger and beating. We tried to escape a second time, managed to be free for several days, but once more were arrested and taken to the Minsk ghetto.

Sheroka Camp

Most of the inhabitants of the Minsk ghetto had already been murdered. "Nothing good awaits us here," said the survivors, and helped us to be transferred to Sheroka, a labor camp for prisoners of war. The camp was under SS administration; the prisoners went to work in small groups. My friend and I found conditions very good. People working outdoors gave us their soup rations and sometimes brought us food which they received from the local peasants. My friend and I caught typhus, but recovered. Sheroka had 600 to 800 Jewish war prisoners, soldiers and officers, and we hoped to remain there until the end. But, one day we were told, "You are going to work in Lodz, Poland." We left, but never reached Lodz; instead we travelled to Sobibor.

Sobibor

On the way to Sobibor, the train stopped in Chelm. A Pole was moving from car to car noting the numbers. We asked him where we were going. He answerd, "To Sobibor, where prisoners are burned." These words became an obsession, but nobody reacted. Incredible! I had arrived from Warsaw and knew nothing of the death camps.

The train left, then stopped again; the night had fallen and the cars opened. Facing us was a poster: SS Sonderkommando Sobibor. The inhabitants of Minsk ghetto were dragged out by the SS officers. "Who is willing to work hard?", one of them asked. A few of us volunteered. The Germans chose eighty people and the others were taken away. I was soon to learn that the Pole of Chelm was right; prisoners were being burned in Sobibor. We were locked up in the camp, and work began the next day. We had to build an underground storage for arms that were taken from the Russians. The prisoners told us what Sobibor meant, and soon a plan of revolt was conceived.

A strong friendship developed between old and new prisoners. Sasha Pechersky prepared details of the uprising; my role was to behead SS Greischutz who commanded the garrison.

Just before October 14, I was sent to camp No. 1 as a carpenter. I was given a well sharpened hatchet by Szmajzner, and I longed to use it. October 14 was a great day. Greischutz entered the tailors' barracks to try a new uniform; I was waiting behind the door. Two blows of the hatchet and my enemy was dead. We took his gun and waited for the signal of the general revolt and our escape. Unfortunately, Frenzel didn't turn up. I had hoped to kill him, too!

At 5:00 P.M., we heard, "Hurrah! hurrah! long live freedom!" I ran, meeting prisoners on the way; I took a rifle and followed them. I can't remember how I jumped over the barbed wire fence and the minefield, but I found myself in the forest. I fell asleep, and woke up at night; I started to run again, as I was still near the camp. I met three other fugitives, among them Boris from Sheroka. We remained in the forest for three or four weeks; at night, we approached villages and asked for bread. Sometimes it was given willingly, more often under threats.

Near the village of Luty, we met another group of fugitives, among them Goldfarb and two Caucasian prisoners of war. We joined Ukrainian partisans. I went out with Goldfarb to fetch some food, and when we came back we found that the two Caucasians and the Jews had been murdered. We ran and met a brigade of Jewish partisans, the Yehiel. We fought together and then joined the Polish army.

When the war ended our detachment numbered one hundred fighters. Later, I left for Israel and founded a family; today I am an officer in the Israeli police.

FROM SUCHE-LIPIE TO SOBIBOR
TESTIMONY OF HAIM LEJST

I was born in Zolkiewka, a village near Lublin. We were half a dozen Jewish families, and my father was a farmer. When war broke out, many Jews came to Zolkiewka, thinking there was less danger in a village.

There were anti-Semites among the Poles, and they included university people; nobody took pity on our tragic situation. Most of the young people, like myself, were arrested and sent to the labor camp of Belzec, we lived with Gypsies and their king Kwek. Life was dreadful; we slept on the floor and we starved.

In the spring of 1942, a man who had escaped from Sonderkommando Belzec told us of the massacres taking place there. Nobody wanted to believe him. In May, 1942, the Jewish population of Suche-Lipie got orders to go to Wysokie, and then to Gorzkow. My family included thirty people, and we walked with the group under the supervision of guards. I managed to escape, and even persuaded a peasant to shelter me for a short time; but other peasants found me, took off my clothes, and left me naked in the forest. I covered myself with the rags of a scarecrow, a straw hat, torn trousers and a linen shirt were my winter clothes. I lived on stolen raw potatoes and became very ill. I learned that some Jews had still remained in Izbica, and decided to join them. On my way, German police stopped me. "Where are you going?" they asked. "To Izbica," I replied. *"Du bist so wie so kaputt,"* (you are doomed anyway) they said, and allowed me to pass.

Spring followed, the last spring for many of us; trucks kept coming to Izbica, taking Jews to Sobibor.

In the camp, fifteen SS and as many Ukrainians were waiting for us. "Men to the right, women to the left," they were shouting; then they selected forty people and I was among them. Later, I wondered if it wouldn't have been better to go to the gas chambers.

From the beginning, I thought of getting rid of the guards and escaping; as a soldier, I knew how to handle weapons. Some prisoners and I intended to attack the guards at lunch time, while they were putting away their guns, but SS Wagner gave me a new job, growing vegetables and flowers. We were to mix the soil with human ashes, in order to obtain a better fertilizer. While I was employed in the garden, Shlomo Podchlebnik of Kolo and Yosl Kopf killed a guard and took his rifle; they escaped with other prisoners, but were recaptured and murdered, together with ten hostages.

On October 14, the revolt erupted. The idea of silent liquidation of the SS and a general escape, realized by Sasha Pechersky, was originally conceived of by a prisoner named Ksil from Krasnystaw, nicknamed Ksil-Kowal (Ksil the blacksmith). He had been killed shortly before October 14, but I don't know why.

Nobody will ever describe our suffering and the courage needed to rebel, with no weapons against armed guards.

During the preparation of the revolt, I acted as liaison agent between camps No. 1 and 2; my job as gardener enabled me to walk from place to place.

My escape and the miseries I suffered later in the forest are like those of all survivors.

FROM CHELM TO SOBIBOR
TESTIMONY OF HAIM TREGER

I was born in Chelm. My wife and two children were murdered, and I was eventually deported to Sobibor.

In September, 1939, Chelm was bombed twice and over 250
people lost their lives. In October, the German army occupied the
town and took hostages away; these hostages were forced to notify
us that all men, aged fifteen to sixty, were to gather in the market
place. We tried to hide, but the SS caught 2,000 of us. After
taking our watches, jewelry and money, the Nazis sent us to
Hrubieszow. As women and children wanted to follow the men,
the SS shot at the crowd. Only 600 reached Hrubieszow, and were
directed towards Sokol, at the Russian-German border. 200 more
people were assassinated on the way. The border guards refused
to let the Jews into Russia, and the SS pushed us into the river;
nearly 400 perished. The survivors were sent to a ghetto and
forced to wear the Jewish armband. We had to salute every
German, and we had no right to wear shoes with leather soles.

When the Russian-German war began, the situation worsened. At first, only Jews from Czechoslovakia came to Chelm; then
Chelm became a training center for Ukrainians who robbed and
terrorized us, with the blessing of the Germans. I lost my wife
first; then all the ghetto children were snatched, with the excuse
that they would be taken care of. I remained alone, desperate,
then was sent to Sobibor. On May 22, 1942, I was locked up in a
cattle train with 200 more people. We waited forty-eight hours
before the train started. Many died on the way and, when we
reached our destination, we were so dazed we couldn't react

to the shouting and beatings of the Nazis. A few men were selected, and the rest destroyed. Compared to Sobibor, our previous life in the ghetto was heaven. We had to build a bakery, as the SS wanted their bread made on the spot. My only hope was to take revenge one day.

The revolt saved more than our lives; it gave us self-confidence. We Jews, the most unhappy people in the world, had beheaded murderers of children. We had put bullets into the dirty skins of those sadists.

The Escape

After the revolt, I ran all night in the forest; with me was a fugitive from Warsaw. We hid during the day and walked at night. Tortured with hunger, we begged bread from peasants, and we slept in barns. Soon the bitter winter overcame us. We begged a peasant to hide us in his attic; my companion was a tailor, and we offered the peasant to make him a suit. The deal was accepted and we worked for a whole week. When the suit was finished, the police arrived. We had a fight, and my friend was killed. I spent the day lying on the ground, and at night I wandered in the forest, looking for partisans. I lived on raw potatoes and I chewed roots of trees.

One morning, after a night spent near a tree, I saw a peasant with a shovel in his hand; I pretended to take a revolver out of my pocket. He screamed and ran away. Another day, a group of Poles began to tease me, a little Jew alone in the forest. I answered back, crying that I was Polish, and asked to be taken to the partisans' headquarters. The ruse paid off, and I was led to officers who accepted me and directed me to their unit. I fought with all my strength, always remembering the martyrs of Sobibor.[1]

[1]Haim Treger returned to Chelm after the war. He married a survivor of Auschwitz and left for Israel where a child was born to them. Treger died in 1969, and his widow gave me this testimony.

MY MEETING WITH THE
SOBIBOR FUGITIVES

TESTIMONY OF ELIAHU LIEBERMAN

My father, Chaim Lieberman, was a fishmonger in Parczew. I was the eldest of seven children. Born in 1910, I joined my father's business after I finished primary school. When war started, I lived in Wola Woroczynska, near Wlodawa. I returned to Parczew during the occupation and, like all Jews, was sent to hard labor.

In the Lipowa camp of Lublin, many Jewish war prisoners were tortured by the Nazis. In a temperature of minus forty degrees centigrade, they were taken barefoot to Biala Podlaska. Two Polish peasants who offered boots to these poor soldiers were shot. 1,500 prisoners left Lipowa, but only 200 reached the village of Dzialy. The survivors were locked in a barn for the night. Most of them died of cold; the others were shot.

The Jews of Parczew and I were sent to bury the bodies. We took them to the Parczew cemetery and wept for them, unaware of the fate awaiting us. One day, 500 to 600 prisoners came to Parczew, and were taken to the synagogue. 200 managed to escape and hide among Jewish families. Some were from Warsaw, others from Lodz. The 400 remaining prisoners were sent to Biala Podlaska and were shot.

The end of 1941 saw the massacre and deportation of the Jews from Parczew. My family was spared at the beginning, but was taken away in August, 1942. In the train that led us to death, a group of young men and I decided to escape. I hid a big knife with which I made a hole in the wall. The train was traveling at full speed and, of the six who escaped, three died falling on the lines. The others were slightly injured.

After many difficulties we met partisans and joined the group of Captain Zemsta of the People's Army. He was a man of forty-five, fond of Jews and, in his unit, we all enjoyed the same rights, whether Jews, Russians or Poles. He also helped Jewish fugitives, and there was a rumor that he was himself of Jewish descent. Then I met Yehiel, a young man of twenty-four, and the fugitives of Sobibor. Many of them were wandering in the forest, and several died fighting with the partisans. I particularly remember Szeftel, and four or five Dutch girls. They knew very little Yiddish, but learned it with us. They were lucky to survive many battles. In Makoszki we were ambushed, and 120 of us lost their lives. We were ordered not to abandon our dead, and hid near them, waiting for the night to fall. We couldn't fight a well-armed enemy. We buried our comrades in the wood.

My mother and two sisters perished in the death camps; another sister was shot, and my brothers died fighting the Germans. Only my father and one sister survived. After the war, I returned to Parczew, but the Polish fascists attacked the Jewish survivors; I organized a Jewish defense group and became its commander. In a skirmish three of us were killed. Finally, I left the country and came to Israel, where I married.[1]

[1]Extract from testimony No. 03 18 24, registered by Joseph Spinc, June 4, 1961.

FROM HRUBIESZOW TO SOBIBOR
TESTIMONY OF JACOB BISKUBICZ

One morning in May, my family and I were taken in a roundup in Hrubieszow and a train took us to Sobibor. Many of us died during the journey and, on our arrival, an officer on the platform was shouting, "Men on one side, women on the other," or "All lying down!" For hours we were on the ground, supervised by the SS. Then eighty people were selected from our convoy of 3,000; the others were sent to a forest to an unknown destination. We were assembled in a barrack with old prisoners and two of us were named kapos.

Memories

Some events are still fresh in my mind. I can see the SS officer, Bauer, supervising the transport of the prisoners' luggage to the depot. He was standing on a truck shouting: *"Noch nicht voll! Noch nicht voll!"* (Not quite full). There was a young mother, running hysterically, looking for her child. Frenzel found him and murdered him by crushing his head against a rail. Wagner used to kill children by kicking them with his boots; he also executed the sick and the babies as soon as they arrived.

The SS and Ukrainians feared a prisoners' uprising. Therefore, when a convoy of prisoners arrived, cars were opened one by one, as the murderers avoided a large crowd. In September, 1943, prisoners from Minsk tried to rebel on their arrival. They threw bottles and stones at the soldiers, but were killed by machine guns. I know of all these events because I worked at the railway station for eight months. During that time, more than 200 of our men were killed. If we were slow at our work, or found a piece of bread in a wagon, we paid for it with our lives. Later I worked in the forest, gathering tree branches. It was equally exhausting.

I couldn't believe in the reality of camp No. 3. One day, I was pushing a wheelbarrow loaded with chlorine and, eager to know what was happening in the camp, I went beyond the limit. I was nearly killed. I was obsessed with the idea of escaping, but could not leave my father. One day, he became ill; I tried to help him with his work, but when he grew weaker, Wagner and Frenzel took him away. I wanted to run after him, but two prisoners held me back; soon I heard a shot.

I watched all escape attempts carefully. The first to succeed was a prisoner who hid in a pack of clothes sent to Germany by the SS. It seems that he left the convoy in Chelm.

The Revolt

The first group of the Liberation committee had ten or twelve members, among them Leon Feldhendler from Zolkiewka. He became the liaison agent between Polish and Minsk Jews who organized the revolt.

My Escape

I was running with a prisoner, David, when we met *Scharführer* Bauer and a truck filled with bottles. A Ukrainian approached him and said, *"Ein Deutsch kaputt!"* Bauer began shooting and killed David. I ran towards camp no. 4 and hid. At night I cut the barbed wires with my knife. For weeks I wandered in the forest, and met a group of partisans. I fought until the Libertaion.

Jacob Biskubicz was born on March 17, 1926 at Hrubieszow; now living in Israel.

FROM ZOLKIEWKA TO SOBIBOR
TESTIMONY OF MOSHE HOCHMAN

At the end of spring, 1942, we learned from peasants that Jews were being murdered in Belzec. It was a Friday evening. I said to my wife who was lighting the Sabbath candles: "Light an extra candle in memory of our dead, and let us say goodbye to each other, as we don't know what is awaiting us." A few days later, we were deported. We walked by the Jewish cemetery, and any more; we are ready to die for *Kiddush Hashem*."[1] They were both murdered and we continued our march. Three young any more; we are ready to die for Kiddush Hashem."[1] They were both murdered and we continued our march. Three young women tried to escape, and lost their lives. A child tried to comfort his father; both were killed. We walked twenty-eight kilometers from Zolkiewka to Krasnystaw. Soon we became a big crowd; I had the impression that the entire Jewish population was there. We were put into a cattle train and left for Sobibor.

In Sobibor

A tall SS officer was waiting and shouting, "Those willing to work, come forward." Eighty men were selected and taken to camp, after being forced to spend twenty-four hours on the ground, guarded by Ukrainians. We were thinking of running away, but how? Even a bird couldn't fly away from here. The camp was surrounded by three rows of barbed wire, and guarded by 200 Ukrainians and SS. A young prisoner thought of starting a fire, with the hope of cutting the wire while the SS were putting the fire out. I was working in the tailors' barracks; the Liberation committee gave us the task of executing Niemann while he was going to the workshop to try on new clothes. The plan worked and, when Niemann was putting on a suit, he was killed with an axe by a Russian prisoner. We wrapped his body in a blanket and hid it.

Survival in the Forest

We managed to cross the barbed wires with a group of eight men, including Leon Feldhendler, and Yosele, the son of the Rabbi of Izbica; there was also the man who killed Niemann. He asked me to remain with him, as he couldn't speak Polish. Together we wandered for many days, until we reached the river. My companion couldn't swim and we had to cross a bridge. We found a field of beetroots, and ate some. We took the road that led to Zolkiewka. Two armed SS officers saw us, *"Hände hoch!"* (Hands up!). We answered, "We are Poles and we are going to Krasnystaw to find work." They searched us and found the beetroots in our pockets. "We shall see if you are Poles, let us go to the police station," they said. I started to run; shots were fired, but I wasn't hit. I reached the village of Papierzyn where I knew a peasant. At dawn, I knocked at his door. "Moshe, where do you come from?", he asked. I told him about Sobibor and he allowed me to spend the day in his barn. When I left him, I went to another farm which I also knew well but the owner told me, "There are police everywhere, and I can't help you." Before I was deported, I had left some possessions with him, but I thought it would be wise not to mention it. I continued to Lublin where I thought I would find partisans but I was unlucky. I had no news from my son and nephews who escaped with me. After the war, I learned that they had perished in the forest.

In Papierzyn, I hid in a peasant's stable for seven months, and left after the Liberation; at last, I was free!

I was the only Jew left in Zolkiewka. I worked with a Polish tailor and earned enough money to buy trousers and a jacket. My employer didn't like me, and I left him. I returned to the place where my Russian companion remained; I learned that the SS had killed him.[2]

[1]The sanctification of God's name.
[2]Testimony taken from *Izkor-Buch*, Chelm, 1954.

FROM CHELM TO SOBIBOR
TESTIMONY OF HAIM POWROZNIK

I was born in Liubomil in 1911 and lived there until the war. I was taken prisoner in 1939, then freed. I went to Chelm and worked in a labor camp.

In February or March, 1943, an SS officer named Weiss came to the camp. He made us line up and walk to the station and we were sent to Sobibor. Some of us tried to escape, but the guards shot at us; however I believe that a few managed to get away. Our convoy included 120 men and sixty women. When we arrived in Sobibor, *Scharführer* Wagner asked for twelve carpenters. I was accepted and sent to camp No. 1. All the rest of our group went to camp No. 3.

In February, 1943 we learned that a guard and two prisoners had escaped and, as a reprisal, the Germans shot 150 workers. The people who ran away had dug a tunnel of thirty meters, but were denounced and executed. In our own camp, we thought that our last hour had come. Frenzel assembled us and made a speech. "Some criminals tried to attack us and paid for their attempt with their lives. You are good workers; you will remain with us, and all will be well." Then he singled out thirty prisoners, and sent them to work in camp No. 3.

In the rest of his testimony Haim Powroznik relates about other attempts at revolt, which have already been narrated by other prisoners.[1]

---

[1]Testimony taken by Ilya Ehrenburg, January 10, 1944 in Chelm. Appeared in *Merder fun Felker*, Moscow, 1945.

FROM KOLO TO SOBIBOR
TESTIMONY OF YEHEZKIEL MENCHE

I was born in Kolo, near Lodz. We were a large family and, with my cousins, numbered at least 200.

In December, 1940, we were deported to Izbica and in 1942, with twenty other relatives, were sent to Sobibor. The convoy consisted of at least 6,000 people, 120 to 150 crammed into each boxcar. Out of that crowd, only forty craftsmen were selected to work. I was chosen as one of the three tailors. SS man Steubel made a speech. "You will all receive plots of land in the Ukraine, and work peacefully. Now, go and change your clothes." He added, "You are going to write to your families that you have arrived safely, and that you are satisfied." Then most of the prisoners went to camp No. 3.

My Memories

I recall some sadistic actions of SS *Oberscharführer* Weiss. One day a prisoner was dressed up as Moses, forced to climb on a table and sing: "Moses, Moses, your brothers are lost; soon they will be finished, and the world will live in peace." We had to fall on our knees and answer, "Amen." The SS man seemed happy with that show.

Weiss also forced us to do the following: we had to find a certain quantity of earth worms, and if one of us was unable to please him, he got twenty-five lashes with a whip. We knew our fate, but couldn't make a decision on how to escape. However, in

October, 1943, we drew up a coherent plan: the mission was to be undertaken by forty men, divided into two groups, and the revolt was fixed for October 14, the first day of the Sukkoth holiday. The group to which I belonged was to liquidate the sixteen SS officers and take their weapons. The second group had to take weapons and uniforms and attack the munition stores. Once the task was achieved, both groups were to join and call all prisoners to revolt and run. Lerner and I were charged with the execution of Greischutz and Klat, while they were trying on new clothes. We got our hatchets on October 13, and everything happened as predicted. Then we went to the camp entrance. The German guards felt that something unusual was taking place, and they started shooting. We weren't armed sufficiently to fight a full battle, so we started running over the barbed wire and ditches. Many of us fell. Out of 600 prisoners I believe that only 100 reached the Parczew forest, on the way from Lublin to Zamosc.

We had many enemies to fight beside the Germans: Ukrainians and Polish fascists. In 1945, only thirty survivors remained. I would like to mention the names of two heroes: Sasha of Minsk, and Feldhendler, who was killed after the Liberation by Polish fascists.

(Testimony gathered by Ilya Ehrenburg, January 10, 1945 at Chelm. Appeared in *Merder fun Felker,* Moscow, 1945.)

FROM USTRZYKI DOLNE TO SOBIBOR
TESTIMONY OF SALOMEA HANNEL

The first roundup of Jews in the village of Ustrzyki Dolne took place in June, 1942; the second one was in the winter. Hundreds of Jews were led to a ravine and executed. One of the SS men said before shooting, "Look how the sun is shining, and how the world is beautiful; and you, you are going to rot."

I was sent to Sobibor with the surviving Jews, on a journey that lasted three days and three nights. Many of us went mad, others died. A child was killed and many women envied the mother, their children were still to suffer. Every time the train stopped, we bought snow from the Poles to quench our thirst; we paid up to 200 zlotys each. We were 300 people.

The Germans took eighteen young men and seven girls; the others went to their death. I remember the day when the gas chambers were out of action; the prisoners ran naked through the camp, while Ukrainian fascists whipped them. Some victims were forced to write to their families and friends that they had arrived safely at their destination.

Work started at five in the morning. Every day there were executions, stealing a piece of butter was punishable by death. If a *Scharführer* gave a prisoner something for doing private work, another Nazi could kill the same prisoner for accepting the gift. The food was atrocious and slow workers were killed. One day, a convoy arrived with many dead, among them some women who had just given birth to children; some of the new-born were still breathing.

128

Three weeks before the revolt of Sobibor, the guard was strengthened and soldiers were seen all over the camp. We heard shots and the *Scharführer* told us that 160 prisoners were executed for attempting to escape. The revolt was organized by the deported Jews of Russia, whose leader was Sasha Pechersky. It was well prepared, and in each workshop, SS men were executed. One of the SS men discovered by accident two dead SS bodies and raised an alrm alerting the Ukrainians and other Germans to organize a defense.

I escaped and reached a village. Since I don't look Jewish, that saved my life. I went to Cracow and mixed with the non-Jewish population.

(Evidence given in 1947, and deposited in Yad Vashem, Jerusalem).

FROM STAW TO SOBIBOR
TESTIMONY OF ZELDA METZ

In 1939, I was fourteen years old and a schoolgirl. I lived with my parents and my two sisters. I am now the only survivor of my family. My village was fifty kilometers from Sobibor. Polish peasants told me that Jews came to Sobibor from all directions, and that they were murdered. "We see the flames of the crematoria from a distance of fifteen kilometers," they used to say. We lived in terror.

On October 22, 1942, the Nazis arrived from Chelm; they announced that our town was to become *Judenrein* (free of Jews), and that we had to go to Wlodawa where a Jewish town was being built. The German, Holzhammer was bribed, and he sent 800 people to Staw; the others went to Wlodawa, then to Sobibor. My family travelled to Staw, where we lived in a labor camp, and worked twelve hours a day. Our food consisted of coffee in the morning, 250 grams of bread at dinner, and soup in the evening. Before our arrival, the Jews from Staw were deported to Sobibor.

We lived in an old mill, under appalling conditions, and typhus caused many deaths. Work was supervised by Holzhammer, who exploited us and always lied. "When you finish working on 20,000 square meters, you will go home," he told us. We knew that home meant Sobibor. The distance from Staw to Sobibor was forty-two kilometers and we were eventually sent there in carts. Some young ones tried to run towards the forest, but they were shot. We reached Sobibor in the evening, and we entered the camp, one family at a time. SS man Wagner selected three men and one woman. He asked the woman to choose eleven girls who could knit; fifteen were chosen including me. Our job was to knit pullovers and socks, and the wool was taken from the prisoners' luggage. The knitted articles were for SS officers Wagner, Frenzel, Niemann, Greishutz, Rost, Wetland and many others. We had Ukrainian guards called the "Black ones," and I remember some of them: Ivan, Volodia and, particularly, Klat.

The Germans had their quarters outside the camp, and were waited on by Ukrainian servants deported from Dnepropetrovsk. SS man Wagner was a ferocious brute, fond of blood, and enjoyed killing at least one prisoner a day. We lived in camp No. 1. Nobody was in camp No. 2; it was the office where Jewish possessions were counted. The prisoners from Western Europe didn't realize that they were in a death camp. They were asked to remember the number of their receipts when they handed over their clothes before leaving for the gas chambers. They innocently believed that they were having a shower. Sometimes the Germans told them not to lose their numbers. We knew the meaning of camp No. 3, but nobody has ever seen it. The camp had only one exit.

We all wanted to escape and to tell the world about the crimes of Sobibor. We believed that if people knew about it, Nazi Germany would be wiped out. We thought that if mankind knew of our martyrdom, we would be admired for our endurance, and revered for our sufferings. I was seventeen years old and refused to die. There were many escape attempts. On one dark night, two of our prisoners managed to cross the barbed wire; twenty workers were shot in reprisal. There was also a similar attempt at the Waldkommando but most were recaptured and executed. In June or July, 1943, we were awakened at midnight, counted and recounted for more than half an hour. Ukrainians formed a circle arround us pointing their machine guns. We heard shots in the distance. We learned later that partisans were trying to liberate us, but without success. Frenzel made a speech. "Last night, bandits tried to approach our camp, but were driven off."

In the summer of 1943, I was working on the construction of camp No. 4. The SS were in a hurry to finish it, with its barracks and bunkers. To speed up the work, the SS formed a Strafkommando (penal commando). We were to eat while running, and do everything while running. Forty to fifty of us died during the construction of the camp.

The Revolt of Camp No. 3

In September, 1943, the guard was strengthened during the day, and SS men occupied the watchtower, armed with machine guns. We heard shots from camp No. 3, and Frenzel told us later that, "The Jews of camp No. 3 wanted to organize a collective escape. They were all executed." They had, indeed, dug a tunnel under the barbed wire, but were betrayed.

Escaping was always in our mind, and we exchanged our thoughts during working hours. We wanted to set the stores on fire, and take advantage of the general panic. Young people who cleaned the boots and rooms of the Nazis every morning wanted to assassinate them in their beds. They were very young, indeed! The greatest pessimists were Dutch and German Jews. They used to say that even if the plot succeeded, they were lost, as they knew no Polish and were in an alien country.

The Revolt

Russian prisoners and Leon Feldhendler organized a massive escape; I didn't know the details of the plan. Niemann and Getzinger were killed in the workshop and the same fate awaited Klat, Beckmann and Steubel. Three SS men escaped: Frenzel, Bauer and Richter. At 5:00 P.M. I was in the yard near Sasha. The barbed wire was already cut; Ukrainians were shooting at us and killed many. Others perished on the minefields, but quite a large number escaped and joined the partisans. Many were murdered by Polish fascists. I hid with peasants and obtained false documents proving that I was an "Aryan." I went to Lvov and resumed a normal life until the end of the war, as if Sobibor never existed.

(Published in *Dokumenty Zbrodni i Meczenstwa*, [Documents on Crime and Martyrdom], Cracow, 1945. The witness now lives in the U.S.A.)

IN THE SHADOW OF SOBIBOR
TESTIMONY OF MICHAEL KNOPFMACHER

I was born in Kolacze, near Lublin, to a family of eight children. The Poles of our region were Orthodox, and less anti-Semitic than the Catholics. When the war started, there was no German police in Kolacze and, therefore, we weren't forced to wear the Jewish armband. But, one day, young Poles caught my father and wanted to punish him for not wearing the armband. They tried to drown him, but old peasants stopped them.

A Request from My Mother

On a winter night in 1941, some Hassidim accompanied a man to our house. He was the rabbi of Radzin, and was sought by the Germans. My mother received him with tears in her eyes and gave him the honor he deserved. The rabbi was very touched, and asked what he could do for her. She answered, "Pray that my sons remain alive, and say kaddish after me." My brother and I are the only survivors of our family, and I still remember my mother's plea to the rabbi.

Sobibor

In March, 1942, all Jews in the region got orders to assemble at Wlodawa. I didn't want to go, and a peasant named Jurczuk offered to employ me as a shepherd. I was fifteen years old. However, one week after my parents left, the peasant told me, "I can't keep you as I am risking my life. Anybody who hides a Jew is punished with death; but if you come to me at night, I shall give you some food." I went into the forest, and slept there, a stick in my hand. Peasants knew I was hiding, but didn't denounce me.

Summer went by. From time to time, peasants brought me news from the Jews of Wlodawa ghetto; I asked them to send my love to my family. One night, hidden in the hay, I heard voices. I was scared, and took the stick I was always carrying. I waited. The voices spoke in Yiddish and, among them, I recognized my brother and one of my sisters. They were saying that people were being rounded up in Wlodawa, being killed or sent to Sobibor. Some managed to escape into the forest. But how can people exist in the forest in the winter? One day, in a peasant's farm, I met Romiach, the male nurse in our village. "Don't let him go," he said to the peasant. "We shall take him to the police, and exchange him for sugar and salt." The peasant answered, "No, he is our little Jew, I shall let him go."

A group of fugitives from Parczew had stopped in the forest. The gendarmes cut off the men's beards, undressed everyone, and exchanged their clothes for butter. Then they started to shoot at the group; only a few survived. Then, together with my brother and sister, I made up my mind to join my parents in the camp of Adampole. We couldn't spend the winter in the forest.

In the Train to Sobibor

When we arrived at Adampole, I learned that my grandmother was very ill and had remained in Wlodawa. I put on a peasant's cap and went to see her. It was Friday and many peasants were travelling to the mill of Wlodawa. One of them took me in his cart; on the way, SS asked us, "Polak?" and we answered, "Yes, Polak." In Wlodawa, I saw a group of Jews surrounded by SS. I continued on my way with the peasants in the direction of the mill and reached my uncle's house. Nobody was there but in the next apartment, I found my grandmother in bed. She was very sick and asked for some water. I didn't know what to do; I wanted to return to Adampole, but the peasant with his cart was gone. Germans stopped me. "Jude?" I answered, "Polak." A Pole who was passing by said, "He is a Jew." One German asked the other, "What shall we do?" The second replied, "Shoot him." At that moment when they were ready to kill me, a group of SS arrived, leading some Jews. They made me join them and we all went to the school in Solna Street. That same afternoon, some boxcars arrived; sick people and children piled up on them and we left.

On the way, I met Shlomo Lemberger, nicknamed Shlomo Doctor, because he always carried medicines and bandages. He said, "Stay with me; we are going to Sobibor, but we shall try to escape. Don't move now, they kill on the spot." Shlomo and I got near a window and removed the bars. He jumped first and I followed him. We wanted to reach the forest and hide, and then to return to Adampole. In the distance we saw a group of Nazis walking along the tracks. I later learned that others had tried to escape, but that only a few survived. We lost our way in the forest and, instead of reaching Adampole, we arrived at Orchow station, the point of departure for Sobibor. We retraced our steps and walked a long time before reaching Adampole. My family thought I was dead. We bought some revolvers from peasants, went to the forest where we found the partisans of Lichtenszein, and joined them. In August, 1943, we reached the Bug River. Poles betrayed us to the Nazis. There was a struggle, the SS ran away, and we crossed the river. We joined the Molotov brigade and were happy because food was plentiful. Peasants feared us and fed us. My cousin, Moshe Zelikowitz, escaped the massacre of Adampole, which took place on September 13, 1943. He reported that Nazis from Wlodawa had shot my mother and her six children in the courtyard of the house. My father was stabbed in the stable.

Our partisans fought great battles. Later I joined the Red Army, and was involved in battles on German soil. In 1947, I left for Israel.

WHO WERE THEY?

TESTIMONIES OF ESTHER RAAB
AND SAMUEL LERER

Esther Raab and Samuel Lerer were witnesses at two trials of war criminals. The first took place in Berlin in 1950, where Erich Bauer, who belonged to the SS Staff of the Sobibor death camp, was brought to trial. The second was in Hagen in 1964, where ten other SS men of the Sobibor death camp were tried. Thanks to the testimonies of these two witnesses, the Berlin court prepared their accusations, relating how trainloads of Jews were brought to Sobibor from towns in Poland and several countries of western Europe. As previously stated, the trial took place in Berlin and, on May 8, 1950 Bauer was sentenced to life imprisonment. Esther Raab and Samuel Lerer recognized this SS man while walking on a crowded street in Kreutzberg.

Who was this SS man who killed thousands of men, women and children with gas and gun? As we shall see, he grew up in normal conditions and was a streetcar conductor in Berlin. Erich Bauer was born in 1900. He was one of the three children of a furniture upholsterer and decorator. He attended public school and, at the age of fourteen started to learn mechanics. In 1918 he was mobilized to fight in the First World War in France. After the war he returned to Berlin, learned to drive, and was intermittently employed from 1933 to 1942. In the spring of 1942, he was sent to Lublin, Poland, as a driver, he claims, to some high rank SS officer. Later, he claims, he was sent to Sobibor, again to be employed only as a driver. He remained in Sobibor until the fall of 1943. In December of that year, he was sent to Trieste,

136

Italy, where again, according to his own testimony, he was employed as a driver. As already stated, near Trieste was San Saba, the extermination camp in Italy where the Operation Reinhard men were sent after the liquidation of the extermination camps in Poland, Belzec, Sobibor, and Treblinka. In April, 1945, Bauer was in an American Prisoner of War camp for a short time. In 1946 he returned to Berlin and, on July 30, 1949, was "denazified" by a special commission. Of course, he did not mention his activities in Sobibor nor his membership in SA, which he had held since 1933.

Here are the statements justifying Bauer's life sentence, based on the testimonies of the two survivors, Esther Raab and Samuel Lerer. "His appearance in the camp evoked terrible fear in all the prisoners, as it meant beatings and tortures for them." The following cases show that the defendant exploited every opportunity to humiliate, mistreat, and, finally, murder the prisoners.

There are eleven counts on which Bauer was condemned to life imprisonement.

1. Activity as *Gasmeister*. On the arrival of every transport, after the deportees were undressed, the accused (known by his nickname *Badmeister)* conducted the newcomers to the gas chambers. He marched in front of the prisoners or beside them, beating them with a stick to hasten their march. In camp number 3, he alone directed the gassing extermination of the people.

2. Hair cutting before extermination. After the inspection of SS Chief Himmler, an order was issued to cut the hair of women prisoners. Jewish youngsters were ordered to do it in the vicinity of camp number 3, where Bauer was often present.

3. Shooting of sick prisoners. On the arrival of smaller convoys, when the gassing was not "worthy" to be undertaken, or when the deportees were too weak to walk, due to injuries received during the voyage, they were shot on the spot. The accused, Bauer, helped the *Lagerführer* Gomerski and other SS men with the shooting.

4. Gassing of 300 young women. While Himmler visited Sobibor, the accused Bauer selected 200-300 particularly beautiful girls for gassing.

5. Dogs directed to attack prisoners. After the gassing of a trainload of prisoners, their jewelry, clothes and other valuables

were collected in wagons to be sent to Germany. If the work was not done fast enough, the defendant ordered two attack dogs, kept specifically for that purpose, to bite viciously and to hurt the working prisoners.

6. Transport from Majdanek. A transport of about 1500 men arrived from Majdanek. As the gas chambers of Sobibor were out of order, the men had to wait for their death. Many died of starvation. The others, who were given some food, were fired upon by Bauer and other SS men, as they ran to get it. Bauer killed at least four or five of these unarmed men in this way.

7. Beating the prisoner, Samuel Lerer. The defendant, Bauer ordered the witness, Samuel Lerer, to fill his car with gasoline. Lerer spilled a few drops while doing so, and this so irritated Bauer that he beat him with his whip and kicked him. After this incident, the witness could not walk normally for several days.

8. Beating and torturing the youngster, Max. There were horses in the camp. Bauer accused Max, a youngster of about fourteen, of hitting one of these horses. He and other SS men beat the boy so viciously that he fainted. Then he was beaten again to such an extent that he was incapable of further work and was sent to camp number 3 where he was shot.

9. Shooting prisoners on their arrival. The prisoners who were deported from Poland or the Ukraine knew, or at least suspected, what awaited them. They sometimes refused to leave the train, so Bauer, who was often present at the arrivals, shot the prisoners or beat them with whips or sticks for their disobedience.

10. Shooting of prisoners who revolted. Prisoners who worked in a kommando outside of the camp killed their Ukrainian guard as they went for water. Some of these prisoners were shot on the spot, while others were brought to the camp and executed in the presence of all the inmates, to serve as a warning.

11. Murder of two youngsters. The defendant, Bauer, was driving a truck through the camp. Two young prisoners, aged about seventeen or eighteen, were pushing a heavily loaded wagon and were in his way. Bauer grew irritated that they did not clear the path quickly enough, so he jumped from his car and shot them both to death.

It is purely by accident that the murderer of thousands and thousands of unarmed people was arrested and brought to trial. How many others like him were never traced?

THE REVOLT

TESTIMONY OF MOSHE BAHIR

In February, 1941, the first deportation was carried out of Jews of Plotsk, the town where our family lived. And I, a boy of thirteen and a half, grew up in one day. The happy days of my youth in the bosom of my family seemed so far away—my room, the bookcase, the warm bed with its turned-down blanket in which I so loved to wrap myself. It all seemed like a sweet dream that I had once dreamed, many years before.

The terrible days of the deportation came upon us like a thief in the night. In our house there still prevailed the joy of family reunion, for my father had returned from German captivity. My father, Aryeh-Leibel Shklarek, had been drafted into the Polish army about two weeks before the war broke out. Before the cease-fire, he had been taken prisoner, along with his entire unit, by the mighty army of Hitler, which crushed and trampled everything which stood in its way. For about a year he remained in a German village, engaged in agricultural labor in exchange for food and reasonably fair treatment. After this all the prisoners were concentrated in camps. The Jews among them were isolated in a separate camp and, after a short time, they were loaded onto freight trains and taken to Poland. In the camp and on the train they suffered from the brutal treatment of the German guards until they arrived, weak and hungry, at the outskirts of Lublin. There, the officer in charge of the transport tried to extort ransom from the local *Judenrat* in exchange for each one of the prisoners, and when his wicked scheme failed his soldiers carried out a great massacre of the wretched throng under his cruel command. Only

139

a few of the prisoners from the first transport survived. My father was fortunate enough to be included in the second transport, which passed through similarly dreadful experiences but, finally, he succeeded in coming home to our family. There was no end to our joy, until that morning in February, 1941.

In the early hours of that morning the house shuddered from violent knocks on the door and from the savage cries of the Germans, "Filthy Jews, outside!" Within a few moments we found ourselves huddled together in a crowd of the town's Jews on Sheroka Street. With the help of the *Volksdeutsche* and with cruel blows and many murders, they loaded the assembled ones onto trucks, crowding them tightly, and the long convoy drove out of town. We were not permitted to take anything with us, not even something else to wear other than what we had put on in our terrified haste.

The Torture Road to Chenstokhov

On the same day, after hours of difficult traveling, the trucks came to a stop in the midst of Dzialdowo camp, at the entrance to the town of Mlawa. Two rows of Germans, equipped with clubs and whips, stood in a line several tens of meters long, extending from the trucks to the camp gate. We were ordered to jump out of the trucks and run through the gauntlet towards the gate. Before the first ones to jump had managed to set foot on the torture-pass, the clubs and whips flew and a torrent of blows rained down on the runners' heads. With difficulty and desperate haste, each one hurried to reach the camp gate, people falling and being trampled under their brothers' feet in their frantic race. Only an isolated few managed to get through the gate without being wounded by the blows and lashes of the Germans. In the aftermath of this act of terror, scores of slain bodies were left lying and were buried next to the single privy which was provided for the men and women who lived in the camp. The hundreds of wounded and injured lay without any medical care in the stables that were full of mud and dung, and into which we had been squeezed and packed without room enough to free our aching limbs. In this camp we endured days of torment and distress, thirst and hunger. Under these conditions, one of the women went into labor and brought into the world a Jewish baby, destined for pain and destruction.

After several days we were ordered to line up in formation. After painstaking and embarrassing inspections and searches for silver, gold, and jewelry, when we all stood naked in the bitter cold, each one of us received forty zlotys — a sum which would with difficulty suffice to buy a loaf of bread — and again we were loaded onto trucks, in which we were taken to the town of Chenstokhov.

For the first time since the outbreak of the war we were privileged to get a warm and humane welcome from the Jews of that town, who put the study-houses and schools at our disposal for our lodging, set up soup kitchens and distributed food to us without compensation. This brotherly aid eased our situation and strengthened our broken spirits.

From Komarov to Sobibor

The ability of the town's Jews to feed us was, it seems, limited, and their good will alone was not good enough to satisfy the hungry. The food rations decreased from day to day, the soup grew more watery, and signs of famine began to appear among us. We were not allowed to accept any sort of work, and with nothing to do degeneration began to gnaw at our insides. I did, however, succeed in being taken on as an apprentice by Levkovich, the barber. In the afternoon, father would bring me a little thin soup, and this would be my daily food ration until the afternoon of the next day. And so our situation grew more serious from day to day, until we decided to look for some way out to better our lives.

Rumors reached us that in the town of Zamosc life was satisfactory. We set out on the road, but when we came to the town we encountered the *Judenrat's* emphatic refusal to accept more Jews into their community. With no alternative, we continued our wanderings until we came to Komarov. It seemed to us that this little town was outside the area of the German occupation. Life there was as it had been in the "good old days" before the war; the shops were open and the Jews went on with their former businesses. Here, too, we were welcomed warmly and with an open Jewish heart. No longer did we know hunger; food was supplied to

141

us from the kitchen which had been set up to feed the refugees, but the problem of housing weighed heavily on our lives. Together with about thirty other families, we found refuge in the synagogue, and to us fell the place of honor — the pulpit.

Father found work at the airport which the Germans had built some twelve kilometers from the town. He made his way to and from work on foot. Sometimes he managed to bring home with him a bundle of wood to use for cooking. I, too, found work, on a peasant's farm in a village eight kilometers from Komarov. At first I worked in the pasture, and afterwards was given all kinds of duties in the house and field. Like Father, I made my way there and back on foot, but I was pleased with my lot because, from time to time, I could carry to my family on my thin shoulders a few kilos of potatoes, and this was then a treasure worth more than gold.

On the eve of 1942 came the turn for the worse. The Germans prohibited the Jews from going outside the town and I was forced to return "home." Father continued his forced labor, but he was unable to bring back with him even one piece of wood. The situation of the town's Jews worsened and they could no longer afford to feed us. Hunger stood on our doorsteps, and with it came despair and filth for those who lived in the synagogue. There was no escape from the lice that found their way from the families stretched out on the floor to the pulpit, where we lived. An epidemic of typhus broke out, and it struck me as well. The local hospital was full to bursting, and only after several days of illness did they succeed in hospitalizing me, thanks to connections and strenuous efforts. Even in the hospital my lot did not improve. The Gentile patients received decent care, while no one paid any attention to the Jews. I conquered the sickness by the force of my will, for it was strong, and I returned to my family. My parents were unable to supply me with the food necessary for my full recovery. I saw them tormented and suffering — but all this was nothing compared to our sufferings in the days soon to come, the full, terrible meaning of which we could not even imagine.

On Thursday, April 16, we were ordered by the Germans and their Ukrainian assistants to get up early in the morning and assemble in the market square. Thousands of Jews — men, women and children, old people and youngsters — crowded in from all sides, as the Germans urged them on with cruel blows, shouts and curses. After many hours of standing fearfully in place, the order was given for all working men to be concentrated separately, since they were useful to the German war effort. Among these was my father. From the moment when he was taken from us we never saw him again. My younger brother, Judah, who had the appearance of a true Aryan, had gone out the day before the deportation to work in the village of Rozov, in the area of Zamosc. I never saw him again, either. I, too, could have slipped away and escaped, but I preferred to stay with Mother and my little brother in order to help.

Towards evening they took us in trucks to the train station at Zamosc. The next day we were crammed into freight cars and in the evening the train left, with the whole mob guarded by Ukrainians. Three days and three nights the train crept along, without our being given any food or drinking water. On the evening of the third day the train stopped at a small station at which hung a sign: Sobibor. At that time we did not know the significance of that name. Of that entire transport, which numbered some 2500 souls, only I remained alive.

Sobibor

The small station was located in an area of desolate forest, with no settlement nearby, about 40 kilometers east of the town of Chelm, in the direction of the Bug River. On April 20, 1942, we pulled up to the station house. Next to the name Sobibor the sign announced in bold letters: S. S. Sonderkommando.

Behind the hut extended barbed wire fences which were swallowed up in the tangle of trees. Behind the fence were huge piles of bundles and various personal belongings, flames of fire and pillars of smoke which arose from within the camp and, with their flickering light, tried to brighten the evening twilight, and, above all, the smell of charred flesh which filled the air. It seemed that in those moments everyone sensed that this would be his last stop on earth.

The camp gate opened wide before us. The prolonged whistle of the locomotive heralded our arrival. After a few moments we found ourselves within the camp compound. Smartly uniformed German officers met us. They rushed about before the closed freight cars and rained orders on the black-garbed Ukrainians. These stood like a flock of ravens searching for prey, ready to do their despicable work. Suddenly everyone grew silent and the order crashed like thunder, "Open them up!"

The doors gaped open. With savage fury the Ukrainians assaulted the people. With shouts, curses and whiplashing they got us out of the cars. The sound of weeping and wailing was drowned out in the general commotion.

After a short time all of us stood in orderly rows waiting for what was to come. At some distance from us we gazed at nice little houses, built in unmistakably German style, adorned with gaily comic names. To our left stretched the narrow railroad tracks and upon them was a long line of cars.

With great zeal and precision they began the *Selektion*. The healthy males, the women and the children were put in a separate group — towards the cabins. The old and weak were ordered to march over to the trains and to get inside them. The feeble ones and, with them, the bodies of those who had been unable to withstand the hardships of the road and had lost their lives — these were dragged to the freight cars and thrown inside. It was said that they were bringing these piles of the living and the dead to the "Lazaret" — that is, the "hospital" — in order to receive proper care. The cars left on their short journey. This Lazaret was located about 200 meters from the place where we stood. It was a wretched little shack — and behind it was a giant pit in a young forest. When the line of cars reached the edge of the pit their cargo was unloaded by the "bandagers" — armed Ukrainians thirsty for blood. At the command of *Oberscharführer* Bredov, the cargo was dumped into the pit amidst a shower of bullets fired towards the fallen by the "bandagers," who had been ordered to make sure that no one survived.

We were taken to Lager No. 1. Here was the supreme commander, *Oberscharführer* Gustav Wagner. Among his other duties was conducting the registry of victims and separating the men, who were placed in rows on the right side, from the women and children, who were sent to the left. He chose fifty men for work, while the rest, together with the women and children, he sent straight to Lager No. 3, about 800 meters from us; in it was the "bathhouse" — that is, the gas chambers, hidden in the thickness of the trees.

I walked with my mother and my little brother towards the gas chambers. As we were going through the gate of Lager No. 1, Wagner suddenly came up to me, separated me from my mother and brother, and brought me back to the formation of the fifty men. I managed to catch a fleeting glimpse of my dear ones as they went far away from me and disappeared into the tangle of trees. After that, I never saw them again.

The Work Procedures

The lives and work procedures of those performing various services were planned with German precision and in accordance with the regularity of the transports which arrived at Sobibor.

On loading days our work lasted from five o'clock in the morning to twelve midnight, and everything was done while running and with abnormal zeal, under the blows of those in charge of us. On our way to work, while carrying a heavy load on our shoulders, we were forced to run between two rows of Germans and Ukrainians, armed with whips and clubs, and to endure the hard blows of our taskmasters. We went through this torture-path again at twelve noon, as we hurried to receive our only cooked-food ration of the day, a hunger-ration that barely kept us on our feet. But what won't a man do to hold his ground? The lucky ones among us who worked at arranging the belongings of the people on the transports who had been destroyed, sometimes succeded in finding boxes of canned food or other foodstuffs in the bundles and devoured them unseen. Thus they continued to stand up under the hard labor and the blows which poured down on our heads. Those who were fed on only the hunger-rations, however, got weaker from day to day, and their journey to the gas chamber was quicker.

Scharführer Paul Grot was in charge of organizing the "flogging parades" in which we ran between rows of whippers.

On the first day of my stay in camp, my work was to remove the valises, bundles and bags of the myriads of Jews who had preceded our transport and were no longer alive. We loaded all of these belongings on freight cars which went to the camps of Trawniki, Poniatowa and the like. Sobibor camp had one assignment: to destroy as many Jews as possible in the shortest time. Naturally, because of our hard labor and starvation rations, scores of those "fortunate ones" not sent to the gas chambers or the Lazaret pit fell dead every day. The workers' quota was filled by men from the new transports.

To my great good fortune, I was part of the second transport, some of whose members were chosen as "permanent" workers. Before that, they would choose 200 men from each transport to load the belongings and as soon as their work was finished they would send them to the "hospital" or murder them with salvos of shots, and all of them would have one grave in the camp. I, however, was privileged to be counted among the "permanent workers" of the camp.

The Five Lagers of Sobibor

There were five separate camps at Sobibor:

Lager No. 1 served as a place for concentrating all those who were brought to the camp. Here the men were separated from the women and children; here the strong and healthy men were selected and grouped into labor squads. They would wait in this Lager until they were transported to Lager No. 2.

Lager No. 2 — After the thousands of men were brought in, *Oberscharführer* Hermann Michel took a census, counted the men and made a speech in which he promised that, after all the arrangements were completed, they would be sent to the Ukraine to work and would live there until the war ended. Naturally, they had to leave on their journey neat and clean and, therefore, they were ordered to strip and were taken to Lager No. 3. Prior to this, they handed over all valuables, gold and silver, to the Germans, who listed each item with strict precision.

Lager No. 3 — the gas chambers.

Lager No. 4 — the place where the Germans and Ukrainians lived.

Lager No. 5 — This camp was erected later, at the end of 1942. This was the place where the "prisoners' squadron," the notorious Strafkommando was. This squadron was engaged in removing trees, clearing the area and preparing it for the construction of

146

underground storehouses for weapons. The commander of this camp was *Oberscharführer* Hubert Gomerski.

Lager 3 was closed on all sides to the prisoners of Sobibor. It was impossible for us to see what was going on in that Lager because of the grove of pine trees which surrounded it. We saw only the roof of the "bathhouse" which protruded through the trees. Thus we saw the murderous face of *Oberscharführer* Bauer, who used to stand on the roof of that building and peep through the little window, into the death-chambers.

We all knew what was done inside the building. We knew that Bauer looked through the window in order to regulate the amount of death-gas which streamed through the ducts, which were in the form of an ordinary shower. He was the one who saw the victims suffocating from the gas that was showered upon them and he was the one who ordered that the flow of gas be increased or stopped. And he was the one who used to see the victims in their final agony and in their death. At his order the machinery which opened the floor of the "bathhouse" was activated, and the corpses fell into small carts which took them at first to mass graves and, later when time was short, to cremation ovens instead.

Two hundred Jews worked in the gas chambers Lager. When their weeks of work ended, they, too, were sent to the "bathhouse" and the same number of men from the recently arrived transport was brought in to take their place. This substitution of men continued until the end of 1942. Then the Germans decided to employ permanent workers, instead, in order to spare themselves the work of training and to ensure a swift and efficient performance of the necessary tasks.

The meager food portions to the workers of Lager 3 were supplied by our kitchen in Lager 1. Ten men from our work group used to bring the pails of watery soup to the gate of Lager No. 3, leave them there and take the empty pails back to Lager 1. All of this was done twice a day at a hasty run, accompanied by lashes from the guards. Since there were occasions on which the workers of the two Lagers would meet face to face and, as a result of these unfortunate meetings our men would be taken straight to the gas chambers in Lager 3, this nightmarish work could mean destruction for our men, who never knew if they would succeed in returning to their "home" from this cursed gate of Hell. I remember one incident that happened to a group of our comrades: one day several of them were ordered to roll barrels of chlorine towards the death camp. They went out hastily, spurred on by blows from their guards, and when they arrived with the barrels at the border of Lager 3 the gate opened and the Jews who worked at the crematoria came to meet them to get the chlorine. The men of our camp were ready to return, but, suddenly, *Oberscharführer* Bolander appeared and ordered those who had brought the barrels to join those who had met them at Lager 3. We saw them no more.

In spite of the strict supervision, from time to time we managed to make contact with the Jews in camp 3. Sometimes we would find notes stuck to the sides of the empty buckets that were brought back from the gate. In these notes the men who worked at burning the bodies described what went on at Lager No. 3. One note told of a bloodstain which could not, by any means, be cleaned or scraped from the floor of the gas chamber. Finally, experts came and determined that the stain had been absorbed into the chamber's floorboards after a group of pregnant women had been poisoned and one of them had given birth while the gas was streaming into the chamber. The poison gas had mingled with the mother's blood and had created the indelible stain. Another note said that, one day, the workers were ordered to replace a few floorboards because several fragments of ears, cheeks and hands had become embedded in them.

Thus we learned that the Jews who worked in the crematoria had a few times tried to rebel and had even made desperate attempts to escape from the camp. These attempts failed, and all the workers were immediately sent to the gas chambers after enduring hellish torture. One unsuccessful escape attempt, daring and well-planned, occurred about three months before the great revolt at Sobibor. Over many weeks, the crematoria workers had dug a tunnel from the shed where they lived towards the barbed wire fences of the camp. They did their work with spoons and their fingernails, lacking digging tools. They scattered the earth in the crematoria, mixed with the ashes of the victims. When the work was almost finished and they had only one meter left to dig, the Germans discovered it. In their murderous rage, they subjected those who participated in the

148

plan to indescribable tortures and sent the whole group of workers to the ovens.

The Murder Crew

At Sobibor, a group of trained murderers was always at work, carrying out the "sublime" tasks imposed on them, in most cases with exceeding cruelty.

The first one of them whom I encountered when we came to camp was *Oberscharführer* Gustav Wagner, who was, in fact, the supreme commander at Sobibor. He was a handsome man, tall and blond — a pure "Aryan." In civilian life he was, no doubt, a well-mannered man; at Sobibor he was a beast of prey.

His duties at camp were many and varied: counting the Jews who arrived in the transports, selecting those capable to work, concentrating the valuables of the arrivals. He was responsible for all of the administrative work in the camp and, in particular, — sending the myriads to the gas chambers.

His unfettered cruelty knew no bounds, and the horror-dramas that he enacted give me nightmares to this day. He would snatch babies from their mothers' arms and tear them to pieces in his hands. I saw him beat two men to death with his rifle butt because they did not understand his directions properly, and this because they did not understand German. One night there arrived in camp a group of youths aged fifteen or sixteen, whose primary task was to cut the women's hair before they entered the gas chambers. The head of the group was one Abraham. After a long and arduous work day, this young man collapsed on his pallet and fell asleep. Suddenly Wagner came into our hut and Abraham did not hear him call to stand up at once before him. Furiously, he pulled Abraham, naked off of his bed, and began to beat him all over the body. When Wagner grew weary of the blows he took out his revolver and killed him on the spot. This atrocious spectacle was carried out before all of us including Abraham's younger brother.

Every time Wagner riveted his glance on a group of prisoners who were ready to leave for work and he found somebody whom, for some reason, he did not like, at that very moment he decided his fate; he would pluck this Jew out of the rows of the formation and personally escort him to the Lazaret. After some time, he would come back in high spirits. His victim would not return from there.

More than once, in conversations among the few remaining survivors of Sobibor, when we mention Wagner, nearly all of us state with certainty that, if he had stayed in camp until the end, the revolt would not have broken out, or would have failed from the outset.

Scharführer Paul Grot was, without doubt, one of the most ruthless murderers of the team of camp commanders. Grot was the leader of the Ukrainian "columns," between the two rows of whom the camp prisoners were frequently ordered to pass, to be scourged with leaden whips, rubber clubs and all kinds of flagellation-instruments with which the servants of the Nazis, who stood on both sides of the row, were equipped. Grot carried out this task with zeal and pleasure. He had a trusted assistant in this work: his dog, Barry, a wild beast the size of a pony, well trained and obedient to the short, brutal orders of his master. When he heard Grot cry "Jude!", the dog would attack his victim and bite him on his testicles. The bitten man was, of course, no longer able to continue his work, and then Grot would take him aside and ask him in a sympathetic voice, "Poor fellow, what happened to you? Who did such a thing to you? It certainly must be hard for you to keep working, isn't it? Come with me; I'll go with you to the clinic!" And, sure enough, Grot accompanied him, as he accompanied scores of workers every day, to the Lazaret, to the giant grave behind the worn-out hut, where armed Ukrainian "bandagers" greeted the sick and bitten men.

In most cases, these men would place buckets on the heads of the victims, after they made them get into the pit, and would practice shooting, along with Grot, who was, of course, always the most outstanding shot.

Grot would return from the clinic satisfied and gay — and look for more victims. His dog knew his master's temperament and helped him in his murderous pleasures. Sometimes Grot would have himself a joke; he would seize a Jew, give him a bottle of wine and a sausage weighing at least a kilo and order him to devour it in a few minutes. When the "lucky" man succeeded in carrying out this order and staggered from drunkenness, Grot

150

would order him to open his mouth wide and would urinate into his mouth.

After a long period of savage frenzy, Grot suddenly changed for the better. It was said, in camp, that he had fallen in love with a beautiful young Jewish woman from Czechoslovakia named Ruth, and had made her his mistress. At the end of 1942, Grot was transferred to another death camp. The day after he left, Ruth was no longer among the living.

Oberscharführer Hermann Michel was a man of thirty-five or forty, tall, thin, with a delicate face and polished, flowery speech. He treated his servants decently, but his victims rudely and brutally. Because of the slippery-tongued speeches which he delivered to the arrivals at camp, we nicknamed him the "preacher." When a new transport would arrive Hermann would deliver his lying speech, in which he assured the arrivals that this was a transit camp where they would only undergo classification and disinfection, and from here they would be taken to work in the Ukraine until the war was over. In his apartment in the camp there was concentrated the abundant property that the arrivals had brought with them — silver, gold, rings, watches, jewelry and various other valuables. Actually, he was the camp treasurer.

All the transports passed into Hermann's hands; he classified the arrivals, ordered them to strip and instructed them how to arrange their clothing so they would get it back when they came out of the "bathhouse." He would escort the people on the special road that led from Lager No. 2 to the barbers' huts and from there — to the gas chambers. With his tricks and his smooth tongue, Hermann was more dangerous than his comrades in crime.

I have already described the duties of *Oberscharführer* Bauer in camp No. 3, in the gas chambers and their operation. It is difficult to describe his base character. Perhaps it will become clear from the vile joke that I heard from him after I had been at Sobibor for some time, while I was working in the Germans' casino. One day he told a story about the "stupid Jews": A transport of naked women was brought into the "bathhouse." One woman saw Bauer as he stood on the roof, waiting for the doors to be hermetically sealed so that he could order that the gas-taps be opened. The woman stopped the armed soldier who stood by the entrance door and asked him, "What's the officer in uniform doing on the roof? Is something wrong? How can we wash our-selves here inside while they're fixing the roof?" The guard paci-fied her, saying that in just a moment the roof would be fixed and, as for her, she need not hurry to push herself inside; there would be enough room for her, too . . .

This was Bauer's story about the naive Jewess. At the end of his story Bauer dissolved in laughter; he even succeeded in infect-ing the camp commander and the officers around the casino with his laughter.

In 1945, Bauer was sentenced to life imprisonment and is still in jail.

It is hard to forget *Oberscharführer* Karl Bolander, with his athletic body and long hair, who used to go walking half-naked, clad only in training-breeches, carrying a long whip with which he brutally lashed the camp prisoners whome he came upon on his way.

He too, "worked" in Lager 3, in the gas chambers. On his way to lunch he was in the habit of passing by the main gate and swinging a whip with all his strength upon the heads of those who went through — this to increase his appetite for the meal which awaited him.

Once, when I was still working in the Bahnhof-Kommando, the group was accused of carelessness because we had left a window open on one of the train cars. Each one of us was punished with 100 lashes. Bolander was very active in this task. More than once I saw him throwing babies, children, and the sick straight from the freight cars into the cars that went with their load to the Lazaret. He was the one who chose the ten men to deliver the food to the workers in Lager 3. When he had a yen to accompany the group, not one of them would return to us when the task was done.

In December, 1965, a trial of the Sobibor criminals was held in Hagen, West Germany, and among them was Karl Bolander. The writer of these lines was one who testified in that trial. The day after his testimony was presented, Bolander committed suicide by hanging in his detention-cell.

Oberscharführer Gomerski, about thirty to thirty-five years old, tall of stature, with an athletic build and a facial expression that spread terror, supervised the group of workers whom the Germans called Wald-Kommando; it was, in fact, the notorious

Strafkommando. Gomerski was cruel and coarse; he was cruel for pleasure to the workers in his group. He could always find an excuse to bludgeon them murderously with anything that came to hand. Most of the time he used the butt of his rifle, which he never put down, even when he was with his friends at the casino.

He made the workers run to and from work. When they bent over to pick up branches while cutting down trees he enjoyed stabbing them in the buttocks with his pocketknife. From time to time he would complete the number of workers in his Kommando with new men, for never did the full number of workers who had gone out to work with him in the morning return to camp.

According to his assignment, Gomerski was in charge of Lager No. 5, which was just being built. When the pressure of new transports increased, however, his workers would help take the arrivals from the freight cars.

In 1948, Gomerski was brought to trial and sentenced to life-imprisonment. In 1972, he was released from prison in Berlin because of poor health. He was incarcerated for fifteen more years, starting in 1974.

Oberscharführer Paul Bredov, aged forty, a Berliner, was a human beast in the full sense of the word. His direct assignment was to be in charge of Lazaret, but he had additional jobs in camp. His beloved hobby was target-shooting. He had a daily "quota" of shooting and killing fifty Jews, all with his automatic pistol which was never separated from him even for a minute throughout the day.

There were other commanders in camp, and each one of them excelled in murderous treatment of the arrivals, who were brought staight to the gas chambers or the Lazaret, or who were spared for a time for oppressive labor, while being beaten and tortured incessantly and, by and large, eventually murdered by the Germans and their Ukrainian assistants. One of them was *Oberscharführer* Karl Frantzel, of whom I shall speak later.

The head commanders, who were in charge of all of Sobibor and everything done within its bounds, supervised all of these murderers. When I came to the camp the commander was *Sturmbannführer* Wirth; after him came *Haupsturmführer* Franz Reichleitner, and the last of them was *Untersturmführer* Niemann, who was killed on the day of the revolt.

Wirth wore the green uniform of th S.D. He was a mature man, gray-haired and particular about his elegant dress, who would often ride about on his horse, his green cape flapping in the breeze. His appearance in camp cast dread over all of us. Our supervisors began to step up the rhythm of the working and the running, and beat us severely. Even the Germans and Ukrainians would tremble with fright when they saw him coming towards them, and we felt their cowardice well on our flesh. Subsequently, we learned that Wirth was killed by partisans in 1944 in Italy.

Reichleitner, a *Haupsturmführer* in his forties, with an Austrian accent, also dressed with great elegance and his hands were always gloved. He, too, cast fear over the officers and the assigned men. He ran the camp with German precision and, during his time, not a single job was postponed for the coming of transports on the following day. He, himself, appointed his assistants and decided who among them would stay and who would be sent to another camp or to the front.

He remained commander of the camp until Himmler's second visit. In his place arrived *Untersturmführer* Niemann.

Himmler at Sobibor

I was "lucky" to see *Reichsführer* of the SS Heinrich Himmler when he visited Sobibor. The first time he visited the camp was at the end of July, 1942. The camp was operating under an unusually heavy workload. The gas chambers and crematoria were working at full strength. Three transports were arriving each and every day and those who came on them, no matter how many, were liquidated on the same day.

On one of these days *Oberscharführer* Karl Frantzel announced to us during the morning roll-call that the next day we would not go out to our usual work. They were expecting a delegation of high officers, and we had to clean thoroughly the huts where we lived; perhaps they would also want to visit us. We knew that, a day before, several young women had been taken to the casino for a meticulous cleaning of all its corners and to ready it for the delegation. Special delicacies had been prepared in the casino kitchen in honor of the high-ranking guests. They rushed me and my friend Joseph Pines to the officers' cabins to polish their boots.

We were still busy with our work when, through the window, I saw a train with luxurious cars stopping at the train station. It was eleven o'clock in the morning. From one of the cars came *Reichsführer* Heinrich Himmler and after him an entourage of six S.S. officers and three in civilian clothes. Among those accompanying him was Adolf Eichmann. (Their faces are deeply etched in my memory, and after the liberation I identified them from their photographs in newspapers and in various historical institutes.)

Camp commander Franz Reichleitner and his lieutenant, Gustav Wagner, greeted the arrivals. All the dignitaries immediately went to camp No. 3, to the gas chambers. After about an hour, when I went back to the hut where I lived, I saw them again, as they were going straight back from Lager 3 to the train. There, in one of the cars, guests had seen and, also, instructions were given to the camp commander and his staff, who remained with the delegation. After a short time the train left Sobibor.

The camp commander and the whole officers' corps seemed quite upset, primarily because of the guests' refusal to partake of the delicacies that had been prepared for them. In order to dispel their anger and disappointment, they increased the pace of destruction, and streamlined and improved the campaign of mass murder. I and my friend, Joseph Pines, both of us aged fifteen at that time, were transferred to work in the casino. The young Jewish women who had worked there then were taken out the next day to Lager 3.

After a few days, two giant cranes were brought to camp and set up next to the gas chambers. These cranes worked unceasingly, three shifts a day, taking the bodies out of the chambers and transferring them to the new crematoria which had been built nearby.

In the month of February, 1943, Himmler visited Sobibor a second time. Two days before he came there was a great preparation in camp. Wagner selected a hundred men and commanded them to dismantle the hut near Lager 3 in which they cut the women's hair before they went into the gas chambers. From the cabin's walls and other materials a small landing strip was improvised for Himmler's plane and, sure enough, one morning it landed there and Himmler and his staff appeared before his welcomers. On the day of his visit the men of our camp were not taken out to work and they even received holiday food rations. That day I was working under the supervision of Paul Bredov, who was responsible for the casino, at preparing delicacies and egg brandy in honor of the guests.

We were still busy with the preparations when *Unterscharführer* Beckmann burst in and announced that the guests were already returning from their tour and were heading for the casino. The officers were delighted; this time Himmler had accepted the camp commander's invitation to dine with him and his staff.

Bredov was excited to hear the news and ordered me to hurry back to the Jews' huts. Alarmed, I began to run towards the camp where we lived; the camp gate was locked and, by the time the Ukrainian guard opened it for me, the entire party of dignitaries had come within a meter of me. At its head, the monocled figure of Heinrich Himmler stood out, and around him were the officers who had accompanied him on his first visit as well, among them Adolf Eichmann. The men in civilian dress were not with him this time.

Two days after the visit I heard a conversation between Beckmann and Bredov. One said to the other that the visit was designed to mark the completion of the first million Jews destroyed at Sobibor. In this way I learned from their conversation that camp commander Reichleitner got a high medal from Himmler for his efficiency in the work, and that he would be transferred to another death camp.

After the visit, we all found out that, for Himmler's visit, several hundred young Jewish women had been brought to Sobibor from Trawniki camp. They were put into the gas chambers, destroyed, and their bodies taken to the crematoria, all in order to demonstrate to Himmler and his entourage the efficiency of the work of destroying Jews at Sobibor camp.

Incidents of Resistance

About a month after Himmler's visit, Reichleitner's replacement, *Untersturmführer* Niemann arrived at the camp. He began by increasing the pace of destruction. The gas chambers and crematoria operated at all hours of the day. The death factory worked at full steam.

At the beginning of 1943, Leib Feldhendler, son of the rabbi of the small town of Zolkiewka, arrived in camp with a transport of Jews from Izbica. When Leib realized what was happening he began to devise a plan for an organized revolt. Inasmuch as the matter appeared unrealistic, this young Jew, who was a handsome, well-mannered fellow, began by preparing the hearts of the oppressed and downtrodden prisoners of Sobibor by encouraging them and calling them to a struggle for revenge against the murderers of multitudes of the Jewish people. For him, it was decided that their fate should be to fall in battle, while in open opposition, so long as they were not taken to the gas chambers to die by suffocation and burning. His words had great influence, as if a fresh breeze of insurgence and rebellion were blowing through the camp.

Even before this there had been several incidents of resistance. One day, at the end of 1942, a transport of women were brought to the camp. They stood naked, many of them with babies in their arms, before going into the "bathhouse." Suddenly, all of them, together, attacked the guards and began to beat the German and Ukrainian officers with the babies' milk bottles and with their fingernails; they struck and scratched until blood flowed. The assaulted men grew increasingly furious and a salvo of shots was sprayed at the women. Most of them were murdered before they managed to get them into the gas chambers.

Once there was an old Jew who was brought in a transport of thousands, and who did not allow them to drag him forcibly so they threw him into the freight car. By chance, camp commander Franz Reichleitner was present. The Jew declared that he did not believe the lies that had been told to the arrivals about a "hospital, light work and good living conditions." By his own effort he got out of the car, bent down and in his trembling hands scooped up two fistfuls of sand, turned to Karl Frantzl, the S.S. man, and said, "You see how I'm scattering this sand slowly, grain by grain, and it's carried away by the breeze? That's what will happen to you; this whole great Reich of yours will vanish like flying dust and passing smoke!" The old man went along with the whole convoy, reciting "Hear, O Israel," and when he said the words, "the Lord is one," he again turned to Frantzl and slapped him with all his might. The German was about to attack him, but Reichleitner, who was standing by, enjoying the whole performance, said to Frantzl, "I'll settle the account with him. You go on with your job." The camp commander took the old man aside and killed him on the spot, in front of his family and all the people in the convoy.

Among the professionals chosen for various jobs in camp was a Jew about forty, a man from Hrubieszow, an excellent climber who, with his assistant, built the casino and the lodging-houses for the German officers — to the satisfaction of Wagner.

One night in October, 1942, the climber and his assistant, under the cover of pouring rain and thick darkness, crawled towards the barbed wire fences, broke through the fence and fled to the forest. These were the first two to escape from Sobibor since it had been erected.

The next day the climber's entire work group was taken out to be executed. For some reason the camp administration behaved with surprising self-restraint and did not increase their murderous activities. We had all expected a stronger response.

From the Ukrainians we learned that the two escapees were caught after several days and put to death.

One spring day in 1943 the Waldkommando group, about thirty men, went out to its work. Before noon two men, Joseph Kof from Zamosc and Shlomo Podchlebnik from Kalisz, turned to one of the Ukrainian guards and requested permission to go to a nearby well to bring back water for their thirsty comrades. In order to remove all suspicion from his mind they asked him to escort them. When they came to the well, the two of them attacked their guard and killed him. They took his gun and ammunition and escaped from the camp.

When the three were late returning to their group, the remaining guards began to worry about the fate of their companion. They concentrated the Jews of the group under heavy guard, until it should become clear what had happened to the missing men. The Jews, who understood what had occurred and what awaited them, began fleeing in all directions. The Ukrainians opened fire at them. Most of those fleeing were killed and only a solitary few succeeded in escaping. The bodies of those who were killed were brought back to camp, together with the body of the Ukrainian guard. Eleven members of the group were captured alive.

By order of the Germans, the Ukrainians surrounded our camp and concentrated us in a crowded place, with their weapons pointed at us. We were sure that our end was near. We stood, empty-handed, facing our heavily armed guards, yet even so there were some among us who thought of forcible revolt, even given the situation. A young Jewish woman from Holland who was with us passed between the rows and encouraged us to "do what you can to resist." We meant to split up into groups and assault our murderers. We knew that it would be a hopeless battle — but we would fall with honor. I heard the young woman's words and a thrill passed through my body. It was the first time since I had come to the camp that I had heard a battle cry like that from the lips of a prisoner.

The Germans, it seemed, sensed the tension which ran through our ranks. They decided to prevent a head-on confrontation and one of them turned to us with a flowery speech, emphasizing the seriousness of what had occurred, and led all of us to Camp No. 2, where the Jews who had tried to escape were being held. We were summoned to witness their punishment, so that we should hear and be afraid. We arranged ourselves in a semicircle. Before our eyes, the eleven men from the "forest-group" were brought out to be executed. The order to fire was given by Gomerski, the commander of the Waldkommando. All the victims fell with the first salvo. One of them got up on his feet and they fired again. Even this shot didn't kill him. A third salvo of shots put an end to his life.

We went back to our huts. The mood in camp was tense. Various rumors flew through the air. We felt that our end was rapidly approaching.

One day in the month of May, 1943, we were ordered to remain in our huts. We were not taken to work, and this aroused dark forebodings in us. In the afternoon, the Bahnhofkommando was summoned to its usual work at the train station. When the men got to the train a dreadful vision appeared before them. This train had brought the last of the Jews from the Belzec death camp who had been engaged in burning the bodies of those killed in the gas chambers. These Jews, who had lived in the shadow of death for a long time and had gotten used to their situation, aroused fear in the Germans that they were liable to revolt and cause complications for their murderers, and, therefore, the murderers had preferred to eliminate them with their own hands, without the help of the prisoners of Sobibor camp. As was their practice, this time, too, they behaved deceitfully. When the train arrived at Sobibor they did not open all the cars at once, but only one car, from which they removed the passengers, brought them to the Lazaret and shot them dead. And they did as much with the rest of the railroad cars.

The Bahnhofkommando workers were ordered to clean the cars, and inside them found scores of Jews who had poisoned themselves on the way. Their bodies were still warm. In the cars were letters and scraps of paper on which the Jews stated that they had been promised that they were being taken to a new work-place. Some of them revealed to us in their letters that, if it became clear that the Germans had lied, their minds were made up to revolt against their guards. One of the letters, apparently written during the last moments, said:

> The Germans tell us that they are now taking the Jews of Sobibor out to be killed, but we know that they are slaying our comrades now. The third car has already been opened, and immediately thereafter we heard the echos of shots. Whoever finds this letter is requested to warn his comrades. Place no trust in the Germans' lies and smooth tongues. They will trick you just as they tricked us. Rise up and avenge our blood, too. Do to the Germans what we meant to do, but did not succeed in doing, for at the last moment the Germans divided our forces. That is the reason for our failure.

> A Jew who has stayed more than a year in the death camp of Belzec, has worked at burning bodies, and has seen with his own eyes hundreds of thousands of his brother Jews burned, writes this letter to you. We were brought here, they told us, to replace you and work in your place. But these are the last minutes of our lives. Revenge!

These letters from the Jews of Belzec aroused agitation in the camp. We felt that our end, too, was drawing near. Men began to think aloud about revolt and resistance. Feldhendler's sermons were absorbed by many, but, in fact, nobody knew what had to be done and how to organize and carry out a revolt. It was much discussed, but no steps were taken.

To our great distress, it swiftly became clear that someone had taken care to let several Germans know about the affair. One day, Moshe Goberman and ten of his friends, among the leaders of those speaking about the revolt, and who had intended to begin making actual preparations to carry it out, were taken out and killed. This action of the Germans caused despair and discouragement among us. We no longer knew whom to trust in this inferno. The words and whispers ceased.

To all appearances the spirits had been calmed, transports continued to come, the mass destruction went on. But many of us sensed that, below the surface, something was happening. The idea of revolt had captured hearts and even created souls. Perhaps plans were now being prepared for its practical realization?

The Great Revolt

During the summer months of 1943, transports of Jewish prisoners of war from the Russian army began arriving at Sobibor. Their fate was like that of all those who arrived at the camp. At the end of the summer, the Germans chose fifty men from one of the transports to work at Camp No. 5, where underground storehouses had been built. Among these prisoners was an officer, a Russian Jew, named Alexander (Sasha) Pechersky. Everyone who came in contact with him was fascinated by his personality, his strong character, his devotion to his Jewish brethren and his profound hatred for the German destroyers of his people.

Upon coming to the camp he understood immediately what was going on and decided that it was necessary to do the impossible and to save the camp prisoners as long as they were alive.

The idea of revolt was ripe and Sasha began to carry it out. He, himself, found his way to the suitable and trustworthy men and, with great secrecy, he passed his plan on to them.

At this time there were about six hundred Jewish workers in camp, engaged in various tasks. Zero hour had been set for the

14th day of October, at 4:00 P.M. About thirty men had been let in on the secret plans, among them the directors of the workshops. These men invited in the camp officers, minutes apart from one another, to be measured for shoes and suits, to get boots, and so forth. All of this was planned for the last half-hour of work, beginning at 3:30. When the first officer appeared at the workshop, two of the prisoners met him; one struck him on the head with an axe and the other stabbed him with a knife. The rest hurried to remove the body and clean up the bloodstains, for another officer had been invited to this workshop. Everything was done rapidly and with great precision. At the same time, the telephone lines were cut so that they could not easily be repaired. Another group cut the electric wires that ran through three of the barbed wire fences around the camp.

Several minutes before the appointed hour, Judah the barber, as was his daily task, sounded the bugle call which announced the end of the workday in camp. The men began to arrange themselves on the roll call ground, just as they did every day. There was no evidence of any kind in camp. The Ukrainians, too, arranged themselves in another place and waited for the German officer who, for some reason, was late in coming. Only a few men knew that he was no longer among the living. Two Jews in Ukrainian uniforms and another Jew disguised as a German officer set off towards the main gate to get the keys, but they were not there. They got only one key to the small gate nearby. At that moment, ten Jews burst the doors of the munitions warehouse and managed to grab several guns.

Suddenly, a Ukrainian, looking for his commander, appeared at the gate; he was shot and fell to the ground. The Jews began to swarm towards the gate and some of them broke off and ran to the barbed wire fences so as to break through and escape that way. The Ukrainians realized what was happening, but were confused because nobody was there to order them to fire. Nineteen of the twenty-one officers who were in camp that day were destroyed, headed by the commander of Sobibor camp, *Untersturmführer* Niemann. One of the officers survived because he was out of camp that day. Another sensed that something was amiss; he refrained from coming to the workshop where he had been invited and managed to hide himself. When the signal for attack was given, he came out of his hiding place and ordered the Ukrainians to open fire towards the gate. The bodies of the first to fall blocked passage through the small gate, and many of those running to the locked main gate were killed by the Ukrainians' heavy fire.

In spite of these obstacles, some 400 men succeeded in escaping from the camp; about 150 fell there, and about 50, sick and weak, did not try at all to escape.

The End of the Matter

Of the 400 men who escaped, only forty survived, most of whom now live in Israel. During their escape, not a few men stepped on mines which had been hidden alongside the barbed wire fences. A great many were murdered in the forests by Poles; some fell in fighting along with the partisans whom they had joined in the forests.

Leib Feldhandler, who saw his dream of revolt realized, survived, married, and set up a home, but fate was cruel to him. About six months after the liberation he was murdered by Poles in Lublin.

And I — suffered agonizing hardships until the liberation. On the day of the liberation I enlisted in the Polish army and when the war ended I set out on my "escape" and went up to the Holy Land.

Until my last day, the horrors of my time at Sobibor will be with me, as will be the memory of the daring revolt in that camp.

(These memoirs of M. Bahir, which were written in about 1950, were issued by "The Museum of Fighters and Partisans" in Tel Aviv in 1970.)

POSTSCRIPT

Sobibor was one of the smallest Nazi extermination camps and one of the least known. Very little has been written about it, compared with Auschwitz-Birkenau. Most of the prisoners were killed on their arrival; very few survived the uprising of autumn, 1943 and, among the little group of survivors, many perished during the escape.

34,000 Dutch Jews were deported to Sobibor; among them my parents, my young sister and many members of my family. Only nineteen came back to Holland after the war. They were saved by being transferred to another camp or by taking part in the revolt.

Mrs. Miriam Novitch has dedicated many years of her life to tracking the survivors of Sobibor and collecting evidence. Many events are repeatedly narrated in the book, but I believe that Mrs. Novitch was right to report every detail given to her. When so many people died, the recollections of the small handful of survivors take on an inestimable value.

This sober and accurate statement is a remarkable contribution to our knowledge of the Holocaust, and Miriam Novitch deserves, once more, the deep gratitude of all those who are interested in the fate of the Jewish people during the Nazi period. Her work has not only an historical dimension; it strengthens our resolution which is expressed in these two words: Never again!

Louis de Jong
Director of the Royal Institute
of History of the Second World War
Amsterdam, Holland

BIBLIOGRAPHY

Ainsztein, R. *Jewish Resistance in Nazi-Occupied Eastern Europe.* London: Paul Elek, 1974.

Ajzenstein, B. *Resistance in Ghettos and Camps.* Historical Material and Documents. Warsaw: Central Commission for Jewish History, 1966 (in Polish).

Ehrenburg, Ilya. *Murderers of Peoples* (Merder fun Felker), Zamlung II. Moscow: Emes, 1945 (in Yiddish).

The Extermination Camp of Sobibor. Warsaw: Central Commission for Investigation of the Nazi Crimes in Poland, Vol. III, 1947 (in Polish).

Hochman, Moshe. "Sobibor," in *Memorial for Chelm.* Johannesburg, 1954 (in Yiddish).

Jewish Observer and Middle East Review, London, April 1965.

Lukaszkiewicz, Z. *Report on the Investigation of the Nazi Crimes in Poland,* no. 3, 1947 (in Polish).

Pechersky, A. *The Sobibor Revolt.* Moscow: Emes, 1946 (in Yiddish).

Poliakov, Leon. *Harvest of Hate.* New York: Holocaust Library, 1979.

Reder, Rudolf. *Belzec.* Cracow: Central Historical Commission for Jewish History, 1946 (in Polish).

Rutkowski, Adam. "Resistance at the Death Camp of Sobibor." Warsaw: *Bulletin of Jewish Historical Commission,* nos. 65-66, 1968 (in Polish).

"Deportation of the French Jews to Auschwitz/Birkenau and Sobibor." *Le Monde Juif* 57/58 (January-June 1970) (in French).

Sobibor. (The Hague: Information Office of the Dutch Red Cross, 1948 (in Dutch).

"Sobibor." *Sovietish Heimland,* 2, 1964; 10-12, 1968 (in Yiddish).

Szmajzner, Stanislaw. *In the Hell of Sobibor, a Tragedy of a Young Jew.* Rio de Janiero, 1968 (in Portuguese).

Suhl, Yuri. *They Fought Back.* The Story of the Jewish Resistance in Nazi Europe. New York: Crown Publishers, 1967.

Talmant, U.R. "The Insurgents of Sobibor. Some Details by a Survivor." *Resistance Unie,* No. 1. Vienna, 1962 (in German).

Tenenbaum, Joseph. *In Search of a Lost People - Sobibor.* New York: The Beechhurst Press, 1948.

Tomin, V. and A. Sinilnikow. "Return Undesirable, A Documentary Story." *Young Guard.* Moscow, 1964 (in Russian).

Vermehren, Isa. *Voyage Through the Last Act, a Report.* Hamburg: Christian Wegner (in German).

Zimerman-Ginzburg, Slava. "Their Last Trip," *Memorial for Kurow.* Tel Aviv, 1955 (in Yiddish).

Zukerman, Herszel. "From Kurow to Sobibor, Revolt in Sobibor." *Memorial for Kurow."* Tel Aviv, 1955 (in Yiddish).

The illustrations are taken from the archives of the Kibbutz Lohamei Haghettaot, (Kibbutz of Ghetto Fighters), Israel.

ANNEX

Der Kommandeur
der Sicherheitspolizei und des SD
für den Distrikt Lublin
Grenzpolizeikommissariat Chelm

Cholm, den 17.März 1944.

B e r i c h t .

Betrifft: Bandenkampfabzeichen.

Vorgang: Kdr.Befehl Nr.11 vom 11.März 1944,Abs.105.

Anlage: Keine.

In den Nachmittagsstunden des 15.10.1943 unternahmen etwa 300 Häftlinge des Sonderlagers Sobibor,nachdem sie einen Teil der Wachmannschaften entwaffnet und einen SS-Führer,sowie 10 SS-Unterführer ermordet hatten,einen Ausbruchsversuch,der zum Teil gelang.

Vom Grenzpolizeikommissariat Chelm wurde ein Einsatz-kommando nach Sobibor entsendet,dem die nachstehend angeführten SS-Angehörigen beigegeben waren:

SS-Untersturmführer	B e n d a Adalbert,	✓
SS-Hauptscharführer	P r u c k n e r Ludwig,	
SS-Hauptscharführer	B e n z l e r Hermann,	
SS-Oberscharführer	S c h o l z Erich,	✓
SS-Oberscharführer	T h e i m e r Rudolf,	✓
SS-Oberscharführer	S c h l ö g l Konrad und	
SS-Rottenführer	R e i n e l t Adolf	✓

Ausserdem war Wehrmacht und Schutzpolizei aufgeboten. Mit Rücksicht auf die Art die Sonderlagers und dessen Häftlinge, wurde veranlasst,dass die Wehrmacht sofort die Verfolgung der Flüchtigen und die Schutzpolizei die Sicherung des Lagers ausserhalb der Lagerumzäumung aufnahm.

Das vom Grenzpolizeikommissariat Chelm entsandte Ein-satzkommando führte die Durchkämmung der einzelnen Lager inner-halb des Lagers durch. Hierbei wurden die eingesetzten Männer in der Nacht des 15.10.1943 und in den frühen Morgenstunden des 16.10.1943 von den im Lager zurückgehaltenen Häftlingen mehr-mals beschossen. Bei der Durchkämmung des Lagers selbst,musste mehrmals von der Schußwaffe Gebrauch gemacht werden,weil die Häftlinge ihrer Festnahme Widerstand entgegensetzten.Eine grösse-re Anzahl Häftlinge wurde hierbei erschossen,bezw.159 Häft-linge befehlsgemäß behandelt.

Alle Angehörigen des Einsatzkommandos haben sich während der ganzen Aktion bewährt.

Beweis: Bericht an den Kdr.d.Sipo und des SD für den Distrikt Lublin vom 16.1C.1943 - Greko Cholm - B.Nr.285/43 - 8 - .

SS—Untersturmführer

Die Richtigkeit wird bescheinigt:

SS—Hauptsturmführer und Krim.Kom.

Cholm, March 17, 1944

The Commander of the
Security Police and the SD
for the District of Lublin
Border Commissariat of Cholm

REPORT

Re: Struggle against bands.
Event: Commander's Order No. 11 of March 11, 1944, Abs. 105.
Enclosure: None.

In the afternoon hours of October 15, 1944 about 300 prisoners of the Special Lager Sobibor undertook — after having disarmed a part of the guards and killed an SS - Führer [officer] and 10 Unterführer [non-coms] — an escape which partly succeeded.

From the Border Police Post Cholm an Einsatzkommando was despatched including the following SS men:

SS Untersturmführer   B e n d a Adalbert,
SS Hauptscharführer   P r u c k n e r Ludwig,
SS Hauptscharführer   B e n z l e r Hermann,
SS Oberscharführer   S c h o l z Erich,
SS Oberscharführer   T h e i m e r Rudolf,
SS Oberscharführer   S c h l ö g l Konrad, and
SS Rottenführer   R e i n e r t Adolf.

In addition to this were also alerted the Wehrmacht and the Police. In view of the nature of the Special Lager and its prisoners, the Wehrmacht was ordered to organize an immediate posse after the fugitives, and the Police to secure the safety of the Lager outside its fences.

The Einsatzkommando sent from the Border Police Kommissariat in Cholm conducted the mopping up of the inner camps of the Lager. Our men were fired at many times by the prisoners caught in the camp, in the night of October 15, 1943 and in the early hours of October 16, 1943. During the mopping up of the camp itself our men had to use arms because the prisoners resisted their arrest. A great number of prisoners were shot; 159 prisoners were treated according to order.

All the men of the Einsatzkommando were equal to their task.

Evidence: Report to the Commandant of the Sipo / Security Police / and the SD for the District of Lublin, of October 16, 1943. — Greko Cholm — B. No. 285/43.
/ — / Signed: Benda, SS Untersturmführer
For accuracy. / — / Signature illegible, SS Haupsturmführer and Crim. Pol. Comm. L.S.

GERMAN DOCUMENT ON THE REVOLT IN SOBIBOR

REPORT OF THE SECURITY POLICE IN THE LUBLIN DISTRICT — OCTOBER 15, 1943 (City of) Lublin

On October 14, 1943, at about 5:00 P.M., a revolt of Jews in the SS camp Sobibor, twenty-five miles north of Chelm. They overpowered the guards, seized the armory, and after an exchange of shots with the camp garrison, fled in unknown directions. Nine SS men murdered, one SS man missing, two foreign guards shot to death.

Approximately 300 Jews escaped. The remainder were shot to death or are now in camp. Military police and armed forces were notified immediately and took over security of the camp at about 1:00 A.M. The area south and southwest of Sobibor is now being searched by police and armed forces.

(From the Archives of the Polish Ministry of Interior in the Jewish Historical Institute, Warsaw. *Faschismus-Getto-Massenromord*, Berlin, 1961, p. 565).